Annie Ricketson's Journal

THE REMARKABLE VOYAGE OF THE ONLY WOMAN ABOARD A WHALING SHIP WITH HER SEA CAPTAIN HUSBAND AND CREW 1871–1874

Laura Ricketson Doherty

HERITAGE BOOKS
2010

HERITAGE BOOKS

AN IMPRINT OF HERITAGE BOOKS, INC.

Books, CDs, and more—Worldwide

For our listing of thousands of titles see our website
at
www.HeritageBooks.com

Published 2010 by
HERITAGE BOOKS, INC.
Publishing Division
100 Railroad Ave. #104
Westminster, Maryland 21157

*Photographs used to create the cover design are
courtesy of The New Bedford Whaling Museum*

International Standard Book Numbers
Paperbound: 978-0-7884-5048-8
Clothbound: 978-0-7884-8312-7

DEDICATION

This book is dedicated to my parents, Leonard and Mary Ricketson, and to all that they taught me.

Table of Contents

List of Illustrations

Annie Holmes Ricketson, from the archives of The New Bedford Whaling Museum

Captain Daniel Ricketson, from the archives of The New Bedford Whaling Museum

The bark, A.R. Tucker, from the archives of The New Bedford Whaling Museum

Map of the world whaling grounds, 1860, credit to the National Oceanic and Atmospheric Administration/Deparmtment of Commerce

Acknowledgements

I would like to acknowledge

The help and encouragement of my family and friends and, also, the members of the former writers group at The Art Complex Museum in Duxbury.

The helpful staff at The Duxbury Free Library, The Ventress Library in Marshfield, The New Bedford Library, The Kendall Library and The New Bedford Whaling Museum. All of these organizations are located in Massachusetts.

Introduction

Whaling was part of my family's history but it wasn't until my teenage years that I learned whaling captains were sometimes accompanied by their wives. We were touring the Penniman House in Eastham, Massachusetts, when I discovered that Captain Edward Penniman's wife, Betsy Augusta, (whom her husband called "Gustie") not only went with him on his long journeys in search of whales but also, on one occasion, managed to save their ship from certain disaster while her husband was ashore. They were off Patagonia, South America, when a storm blew the ship and crew remaining on board one hundred miles out to sea. Under Gustie's direction, the ship and crew weathered the storm and returned two days, later, to pick up the captain and his crew.

It was Jane Druett in her excellent book, "She Was A Sister Sailor," who introduced me to Annie Ricketson and her journal. The journal was located at the Kendall Whaling Museum in Sharon which, unfortunately, was in the process of being closed down. At that time, I had two concerns: would I eventually be able to gain access to the journal; and, was there a possibility that I was related to Annie Ricketson? Finally, I learned that the museum's contents had been relocated to the Kendall Institute in New Bedford under the auspices of that city's well-known Whaling Museum. Imagine my excitement on the day when I was first shown not only Annie's journal but also the original ship's log.

An answer to my second question came when I visited the New England Geneological Society in Boston. My research confirmed that I am related to Annie through her husband, Daniel, a descendent of William Ricketson as am I.

I have attempted, whenever possible, to keep to the tone of Annie's journal with only occasional grammar corrections or explanations. Although, at times, some of Annie's sentiments and observations are not "politically correct" by today's standards, they most certainly reflect the current sentiment of her time. However, I believe from the many events Annie describes in her journal, that she had a genuine appreciation and liking for the people she met.

Chapter 1

When Annie Holmes Ricketson set off from the docks of New Bedford to accompany her whaling captain husband, Daniel, on a voyage lasting just under three and one half years, she joined a small number of women who, in the mid 1800's, were going to sea. There were many reasons why they went: some because their husbands missed them and either requested or demanded that they join them.

Captain Tom Mellon of the Europa wrote, "I am a married man and love my wife dearly and it takes all of my spare time to write to her for I never tire of writing when I am writing to her." Later, while still at sea, he learned his beloved Kate was about to have a child. He wrote, "I tremble for the result and have got to wait in impatience and anxiety until next fall before I shall know the worst. I cannot loose her. I must not loose her, for it seems to me that I cannot live without her."[1]

Another account tells of a woman forced to endure the difficulties of life at sea by an unsympathetic husband. From the start of her voyage, the poor woman was so sick that she never left her room. Soon, she lost so much weight that not one item of her clothing fitted.

At that time, sailors had a term for this type of debilitating illness. It was called "feeding the fishes". Incredibly, throughout her years at sea, Annie was never seasick.

Other women made the decision to go because they were tired of waiting at home for their husband's return. Increasingly, as the number of whales decreased and the quality of the crew diminished, the voyages lasted longer. Three to five years was common. One young wife cried out after her husband as he left her and their new baby, "I might just as well be a widow." They knew the risks of loosing their loved ones were great - two to one against their returning. There is a reason why the railed platforms built on rooftops in whaling ports came to be known as widows' walks. Many a wife who stood scanning the horizon for her husband's ship experienced the ultimate disappointment.

Not that this practice of women going to sea was universally accepted. There is a story of the daughter of one family in New Bedford whose parents were so opposed to her leaving that they declared her dead and mounted a tombstone with her death listed as the day her ship departed.

Many of the wives who chose to go were ill-equipped to deal with life on a whaling ship. Nothing could have prepared them for the constant dampness, long days, sometimes weeks, of boredom, terrific storms and the lack of female contact. Often, they begged to be left off at the nearest port to find their way home on a returning ship.

But there were others, like Annie, who somehow managed the extremes of the new life they had chosen. Women who may never have seen Boston or New York City were to become more familiar with exotic ports throughout the Pacific. Often, they kept journals which tell of washing, sewing, training servants, and making visits as though they were in the most natural situation in the world.[2] These journals present a picture of daily life on a whaler much more vividly than the official ship logs which concentrated more on weather and whale sightings.

Annie made a total of three or, possibly, four voyages during her marriage to Daniel. This is the story of one of them as documented in her carefully recorded journal and the ship's log. The purpose of this book is to convey the often incredible experiences of Annie's life during this time. Except for occasional corrections in spelling and grammar or explanations

2

*of vocabulary terms no longer in use, this account reflects
Annie's writing as closely as possible. It should be noted that
some of her reactions to different cultures are not what today
would be accepted as politically correct but are a reflection of
the period in which she lived. Also, the scrutiny which whaling
has now come under did not exist during that time in which it
was viewed as an industry vital to the nation's economy and
well-being.*

At 9 am on a sunny May 2, 1871, Annie set off with her
husband from the wharves at the foot of Walnut Street in New
Bedford. She was twenty-nine years old, Daniel thirty-five.
They had been married almost fourteen years. The first entry in
her journal reads, "The pilot boat landed us safe on board my
home for the present."

What were her thoughts as she boarded this new "home"?
The bark, A.R. Tucker, was built in 1851 in Dartmouth,
Massachusetts, not that very far from Fall River, Annie's
birthplace. It was 92.4 feet long and 23.2 feet wide with one
deck, three masts, a square stern and a billet head (a less costly
alternative to the figurehead). Her first impression was, most
likely, that it was neither sleek nor remarkable. However,
although it lacked the grace and speed of a clipper ship, it made
up for this in sturdy seaworthiness.

The Tucker looked very much like all square-rigged whalers.
Even their captains often had trouble telling them apart. In a
later voyage on the Pedro Varela, Daniel called Annie on deck to
help him identify an oncoming vessel. It was only when they
saw the ship's name that they realized that it was the Tucker.
"Quite a joke," Annie wrote, "we did not know her and had been
in her three and one half years!"

Annie was a woman of the Victorian age, a time when many
of her sex cultivated an air of weakness in order to be attractive.
It was thought that "a true woman's heart" should be cheerful,
almost childlike in its pleasure at discovering new things and
filled with sympathy for all. Despite these deliberately
cultivated mannerisms, there is little doubt that Victorian women
could be courageous and resilient when necessary. These
strengths would be especially important to Annie.

Most obvious to her on her arrival must have been that she
was the only woman onboard. As one Captain's wife wrote,

"now am I in the place that is to be my home. All seems so strange. There are so many men and not one woman beside myself."[3]

The crew of the Tucker as it departed New Bedford, that day, were a mixed lot representing many races and countries. According to the Seamans Register there were twenty-three members in all, including Daniel. (He was not the first Ricketson to captain a whaling ship. There is a record of a Captain Ricketson predating the American Revolution.) George Bourne and William Harris, first and second mates were white. John Vanderhoop, third mate, was a Native American from Gay Head (now Aquinnah), Martha's Vineyard, Massachusetts. Others came from Nantucket, Massachusetts; Halifax, Nova Scotia; Guam, Tahita(i), England and Switzerland.

As in every whaling enterprise, their pay depended on the amount of oil returned to port at the end of the voyage. Each crew member was entitled to a certain portion of the ship's profits. This "lay", as it was called, was often notoriously small especially considering their years at sea, unpleasant living conditions and life-threatening work.

For this reason, in addition to the rise of manufacturing jobs and the lure of the West, it was becoming increasingly difficult to recruit dependable crew members. The shipping agents who were in charge of recruitment were often deceitful, deliberately misrepresenting both the conditions of employment and wages. As Annie would eventually discover, these practices often led to desertion or worse, mutiny.

These whalemen had very few rights or privileges whereas Daniel, as captain of the ship, had almost unlimited power. Some of this he delegated to his mates but his was the final responsibility when it came to the safety of the ship and the successful completion of the voyage.

The class of men who served as captain or master of a whaling ship was known to be cool and determined, brave and experienced. Daniel was no exception. At the age of sixteen, he left his family farm in Dartmouth to go to sea. Over the years, he succeeded in working his way up from the lowly position of cabin boy to ship master.

As Annie's journal gives no clue to her reaction to the sights and activities of her first days on board the A.R. Tucker

(perhaps, she was kept busy unpacking and settling in), we can only surmise what she might have seen. Before leaving the dock, the costly work of outfitting the whaleship for its long journey would have been completed. The hull would have been carefully checked, the cooper sheathing repaired and any gap in the outside planking calked. All the spars and sails would have been put in seaworthy condition and any rotted wood replaced and painted. The deck was kept natural but scrubbed clean.

At the time of sailing, the ship was short-handed. The plan was to stop at the Azores to pick up additional sailors. There was plenty of work for those at hand. Food supplies were to be stored away in barrels, tubs or cans. Room needed to be found for additional knocked down containers which would be assembled when needed. All the materials necessary for making repairs during the voyage as well as extra sails and cordage had to be carefully put away.

Each of the four whaleboats on their individual davits (cranes), needed to be equipped for the eagerly awaited hunt. Their oars, masts and sails made available for instant use. Supplies including a keg of water, bread, lantern with candles and small flag for signaling needed to be checked as well as the all-important tools - harpoons, lances, blades, short-handed axes, and stout knives.

Most certainly, early on, Daniel would have addressed his men firmly, laying down the rules of his ship. The men would have been organized into watches and those who were to take part in the whale hunt assigned to each boat. There was a very definite line of command on the Tucker which went as follows: Daniel, as captain, had power over everyone; his first mate, George Bourne, made sure that his orders were carried out and was responsible for keeping the log (it is interesting to note that in some of the records of the Tucker's voyage, Annie is also listed as keeper); second mate was William Harris; third mate, John Vanderhoop, who Annie, in her journal, calls Vanderhoof. The mates commanded the whaleboats during the hunt. Usually, the captain remained on board the ship to direct the hunt, although this was not always the case as we will discover with Daniel.

Next in rank were the boatsteerers or harpooners known for their skill and experience. Theirs was the difficult and dangerous task of attaching the harpoon to the whale after which they would change places with the mate who would go forward to throw the lance(s). In a sea churning with the desperate thrusts of the terrified victims, this was no easy feat.

Other important crew members were the cooper who made and repaired the storage casks; the steward who served Annie, Daniel and his officers at table; a carpenter, blacksmith and cook. The rest of the crew were the foremast hands and were considered to be at the lowest level.

The living quarters on the ship were also occupied according to rank with the highest in back, lowest in front. Daniel and Annie slept in the large stateroom on the starboard side. They had the only bed on board which was strung so that the rocking of the ship was counteracted. Just forward of them, were Daniel's mates who had smaller staterooms with ordinary bunks. Adjoining these rooms was a large area used for a variety of functions including office, living and dining room. There was little privacy midship in the small area of steerage where the middle level members of the crew were assigned. But the conditions of the forecastle, quarters for the rest of the crew, were challenging, at best. The ceiling was low and the only ventilation was from a hole cut in the deck for the ladder which was used to enter or leave.

Anyone who has experienced even the more roomy officers quarters of a whaling ship would not doubt that Annie would have early resolved to spend as much time above board as possible. A special room had been fitted out quite comfortably on deck just for this purpose.

The first two days of the voyage, they had fine weather according to Mr. Bourne's reports in the log. As they traveled away from the familiar shoreline, the seaport's wharves with their splendid assortment of ships, the smoke stacks of the newly built cotton mill and the stately spires of the many churches would have been among the last sights Annie saw.

New Bedford, at that time, was still a colorful and charming city. Just past its heyday, it was known as the whaling capital of the world, having reached its peak prior to the Civil War. Americans had dominated the whaling industry from its very beginning. Financial returns ran the full gamut from unbelievable success and wealth to devastating losses and ruin.

These profits or losses affected everyone involved - the ship owners, their captains, his mates and crew members and, of course, all the various suppliers. Many fortunes were made and, even today, visitors to this historic city can see the impressive homes, banks and businesses built with money from whaling. Recently, there has been an obvious effort to restore these magnificent buildings to their former glory.

When the Tucker was setting out, whaling, although still profitable, had begun to experience a slow and steady decline. Many ships were lost during the Civil War. One interesting aspect of that period was the use of whalers by the North to block Charleston Harbor in South Carolina. The Stone Fleet, as it came to be called, was stripped of its gear, heavily weighted and sunk at the entrance to the harbor. In the very year the Ricketsons began their journey,1871, thirty-three ships were lost to ice in the Arctic of which twenty-two were from New Bedford. Other reasons for the decline were the growing use of petroleum and the superiority of natural gas for illumination.

After the first two days of good weather, conditions deteriorated rapidly. The visibility became so bad that although the crew had already begun to search for whales, they would not have been able to lower the whaleboats even if they had been able to see them. During this time, they traveled from Cape Hatteras to the Charleston Whaling Grounds.

Chapter 2

After two weeks of heavy weather, the sun broke through - just in time for Annie to see a large school of sperm whales. What an impression that first sighting must have been for all of the ship members, especially when the whales spouted (blew out air). One captain's wife describes her first experience at seeing theses spouts as "looking queer to see them throw the white water so high."[4] She continues describing how dark the whales looked in the water, a mass of "flesh, flukes and fins". They were in her view, handsome, quite long and very shiny. "There didn't seem to be much form to their heads and their eyes were small. But, their mouths were large." She thought their hearing was very acute because when they heard the least noise, they sounded (submerged).

About this first sighting, Annie wrote, "we saw a large school of sperm whales and lowered three boats. In about four hours, they brought back three whales and positioned them alongside the ship. Two boats were broken to pieces by the whales."

What happened during those four hours? Who was the first to spot the whales? Most likely, it was one of the two lookouts perched high above the ship in the masts. He would have been watching for whale spouts which can rise to twelve feet and are visible from as far as six miles away.

As soon as that electrifying cry, "There She Blows", was shouted, every crewman would have made himself ready. Daniel would have climbed to the main crow's nest to ensure that the ship was headed for the whales. Once he judged they were close enough, he would order the boats lowered.

As was the custom, the mate in each boat would take the steering oar in the stern with two rowers placed on each side facing him. They depended on him for directions and rowed with their backs to the whales. There is no evidence that Daniel went out on this first hunt. Since there were only three boats lowered, most likely he stayed on board the ship to direct his crew in the whaleboats. This was done by prearranged signals using flags.

The double ended whale boats used in the hunt were about thirty feet long. They were quite shallow and built for speed and seaworthiness. If there were enough wind, sails would have been used to head the boats into the whales. When it was necessary to use the oars, they were quickly stored away and replaced with paddles as they approached their quarry. The harpooner would stand in the bow, waiting.

At this critical moment, during the terror and confusion, it was not unusual for a novice crewman, a greenhand, to jump overboard. Care had to be taken that he didn't overturn the boat when he quickly realized that the water was even more unsafe and tried to reboard.

Once the harpooner succeeded in attaching the harpoon and the whale was fastened by a line to the boat, he would change places with the mate - no small feat in a boat being tossed about on water churned by the violent contortions of an angry whale. Enormous amounts of blood would spurt from the wound. Sharks would begin to gather.

On some hunts, the whale would go into a flurry for a few minutes, turn on its side and die. At other times, it would travel at tremendous speeds to escape its attackers all the while with the attached whaleboat in tow. This was known as the Nantucket Sleigh Ride. Or, it would sound, submerge. There was always the fear that the attacked would become the attacker which was what happened as Annie watched from the ship when two of the whale boats were stoved in by angry whales. Even the ship, itself, was not entirely safe as evidenced in the historical story of the Essex out of Nantucket which was rammed and sunk by an angry whale.

Once he was within three to four feet of his target and despite the wild convulsive movements of his prey, the mate, now in the bow, had to aim for the most vulnerable spot and sink his lances. The lances were flat, oval-shaped steel blades, sharp as a razor, welded to an iron shank six feet long. The attack was either from the front of the back where, because of the position of its eyes, the whale was incapable of seeing. With each wound, the whale would bleed freely and weaken. In its last moments, it went into a flurry, swam in a narrow circle, spouted great amounts of blood and vomited large quantities of undigested squid. With a final lurch, it rolled over with its dorsal fin out of the water. This "finning out" was a sign of death.[5]

Then would begin the difficult labor of bringing the whale, now tons of dead weight, back to the ship. As one whaling captain's wife wrote, "It was curious to see them towing it to the ship. The whale was attached to the boat by a long line and drifted along behind."[6]

If two whales were killed by one boat's crew, they would leave one of them afloat where it died and plant a signal flag called a "waif" to guide searchers. All harpoons were marked with not only the name of the ship but also that of the boat from which it was thrown. The rule was "the marked craft claims the fish so long as it is in the water, dead or alive."[7] Since two of the Tucker's boats had been destroyed during the hunt, Daniel had to arrange to get not only his crew but also the two other whales back to the ship. How he accomplished this is not recorded.

Once they reached the ship, the whales were fastened to it using a large chain attached around the small section of its body just ahead of the flukes. The one undamaged whaling boat was returned to its davit. The other boats would eventually be either repaired or replaced with the tools and supplies brought on board in New Bedford.

Immediately, staging was put in place so that the body of the whale in the water, below, was between it and the ship. Next, began the difficult task of "cutting in." Working with long spades, the captain, his first and second mates, leaned hard against the staging's railings as they began cutting the blubber in long strips which were hoisted up onto the ship and into the hold. The head, which in sperm whales is filled with a higher quality of oil, was cut off and also saved. While, they were occupied with this demanding and difficult work, sharks were continuously circling below them looking for something to eat and not caring whether it was whale or human flesh. When they were finally finished, what was left of the carcass was set adrift much to the delight of the sharks. Remember, there were three whales that these same officers had to cut in.

"I saw them cutting the whales in, such a greasy time I had never witnessed before. The heads were so large and such quantity of oil they took from them. It didn't seem possible they could hold so much," Annie writes. After the blubber was cut, it was put into large black pots supported by a brick furnace (try works) located on the top deck.

"Just before night, they began boiling. This process was called "trying out," Annie continues. "The fire looked very

10

pretty coming out of the long pipes on the try works. It was quite a sight to see." Other reports of this process of trying out were not so favorable. One writer compared it to a scene out of *Dante's Inferno.* Another eyewitness thought the whole scene "weird in the extreme - the black smoke from the burning scraps, red flames, tracing of the masts, spars, and sails brightly lit up, the blood-red reflections from the sea, the diabolical appearances of the stokers and the deck hands."[8] And, Annie though this pretty!

Trying out the blubber was hard, messy work which continued day and night until it was done. Care had to be taken not to burn the scraps or overcook the oil which could affect its color and quality. All of the crew from the captain down to the lowliest deckhand was covered with blood. Their dirty clothes, soaked with sweat and oil, were cold and clammy. Their eyes smarted from the glare of the flames and the acrid cooking smoke. The air was filled with soot. Oil eased up through the toes of the workers who were barefooted while those with shoes squished across the slimy deck. The crew took only the barest minimum of time to eat and sleep. Fatigue set in.

One captain's wife noted that whaling was "very dirty work, that of a slaughterhouse. Boiling always made a mess." But, she observed, "the smell of a dead whale" (which has been likened to that of a bank of seaweed) "was also the smell of money."[9] Many wives who were not acquainted with the tasks involved in whaling quickly remedied their ignorance. They were, as a whole, very aware of the connection between filling the barrels with oil, the eventual success of their voyage and being able to return home. Annie herself observes, the work is "greasy and so smelly it makes me sick but we can get along with all of this, for it will be clean money."

Chapter 3

May 21 While the crew was cutting in the whales, Annie saw a brig bound for Barbados and managed to put letters for home aboard. At sea, it was common practice for letters to be sent by any vessel which seemed likely to arrive home before the sender. These letters were received only after long and irregular intervals. A letter from home that reached a whaler in less time then six months was considered prompt. One wife sent her husband one hundred letters while he was away of which he only received six. These untimely mail deliveries were one of the many difficulties Annie had to endure during her years at sea. And, in at least one instance, their consequence was tragic, as we shall later learn from her journal.

May 22 Annie fell down the stairs which were covered with oil and sprained her ankle. "I had to wear my husband's slippers for sometime afterward."

Although she mentions her sprained ankle, Annie neglects to record a condition which could have been much more seriously affected by such a fall. She was several months pregnant. There is nothing in her journal about this except for one hint but that doesn't appear until the day before her baby is born.

On the day of departure Annie must have known she was pregnant. This makes it all the more remarkable that she chose to go with Daniel at such a crucial time in her life. She had miscarried, once before, in 1867. And yet, she was willing to take the tremendous risk of carrying and eventually giving birth to their first child in totally unknown circumstances.

There was a very good possibility that the baby could be born at sea. Daniel, as captain, was responsible for medical emergencies but it is most certain that these never included childbirth. His basic equipment was a chest of assorted medicines and a book of instructions with symptoms by number to correspond with numbers in the chest. The management of a confinement was not written up in The Sea Captain's Medical Guide. Though the possible complications were well-known, it was tricky to reach port before a crisis. Captain Parker Hempstead Smith of the Nantasket could attest to that. One February, his wife went into labor while they were at sea. "Last night, we had an addition to our ship's company - a baby boy whose weight is eight pounds, a rare thing at sea but fortunately no accident happened," the record reads. In addition to such risky medical care, Annie would be a woman alone on a ship of men at a time in her life when she was most vulnerable.

Two questions are in need of answers: why did she place herself in such a perilous situation; and, why is there no mention of her pregnancy in her journal? One writer has described Annie as able to take "the bitter with the sweet?"[10] Mr. Purrington notes her "genuine gusto" for life and how she "kept a happy ship." One of his comments is particularly telling, "She saw all the sights a traveling lady should see and some she should not have." Her journal gives a strong impression of a basically optimistic woman who took great pleasure, first of all, in her husband and, next, in all of the experiences in which they shared.

As to why she neglected to mention her pregnancy, it may have been the constraints of the Victorian age in which she lived. Or, and this appears more likely the reason, Annie saw herself as a ship's reporter. She wrote with an eye more to recording details and facts with very little of her personal feelings shown. Also, she may have been thinking that her journal would be read by others in the future (as it has) and so censored information which she wanted to be kept private.

By the next morning, on captain's orders, the steward and cabin boy had scrubbed the stairs where Annie had fallen with soap and sand. "I guess it will be the only clean place aboard the ship," Annie writes.

Not one to dwell on the discomfort of her swollen ankle or to be put off by the odor and grease of the ship and its crew, Annie continues to spend much of her time on deck. It was not long before she sights a ship in the distance, "it looks beautiful sailing along the blue water." Although she tried, she was unable to identify what kind of a ship it was. Annie in her writing demonstrates one of the characteristics of a successful traveler - curiosity.

On the next day, another pleasant one, Annie records her impressions, "The crew is at work and about as greasy as the whales, themselves. Although there is plenty of water to keep clean with, everything is sticky. Excepting the stairs."

Finally, the oil from the blubber was ready to be dipped into tanks to cool. Then, it was put into barrels and stowed below deck. When they finished these tasks, the men were given a brief rest until the process of cleaning up began. Everything on deck was covered with scum, blood and oil which needed to be scoured away. This was done with salt water mixed with lye made from the try work's ashes. It was a potent mixture capable of washing away each and every stain until the decks were white as chalk. All of the weapons and tools were washed and stored away, ready for the next hunt. Not much could be done with the sails which remained begrimed with soot. While this was happening, lookouts were already positioned in the mastheads watching for more whales.

It was the last day in May and Daniel had a surprise for Annie. "Guess we'll go ashore, this afternoon," he announced. They were eight miles off the coast of Bermuda at the time. Annie stepped gingerly into the boat to take her position on one end of it. A signal flag had been placed for her to sit on. Once the boat was lowered into the water, four men rowed as Mr. Bourne steered her and Daniel into port.

The reader may ask why the ship moored so far from land. This was often done to prevent the crew from getting to shore and deserting which was a common problem on whalers. And, a consistent one for the Tucker, as we will discover.

Surprisingly, in view of her lengthy accounts of other stopovers, Annie writes very little about Bermuda except that "a prettier place I don't think I ever saw." She and Daniel spent several days, there. It was the first stay on their journey in a tropical climate. One traveler of the time has reported that when he first arrived he was overcome by such a lassitude that he feared he had a fever. Another observed that the tropical habit of relaxation made it a waste of effort to try and make people hurry. Such a way of living must have required a good deal of adaptation for one born and raised in New England.

The crew rowed them to Hamilton Harbor which was well-known for its treacherous rocks, so close to the surface that seamen needed to be on constant alert not to scrape the bottom of their vessels. It was said that bringing a boat into that harbor required strong nerves and keen eyes.

Gibb's Hill Lighthouse was one of the landmarks visible when Annie and Daniel arrived. The pink sand, turquoise water and gardens blooming with all the colors imaginable must have been a welcoming sight after their weeks at sea. It was a land of intense light and unbelievable clarity. Winding roads, often enclosed with high walls covered with flowering vines, wound through the small towns of the island. Most of the houses, built of stone to resist hurricane winds, were freshly white washed or painted in soft pastels. The stately Royal Palms stood like windmills reaching toward the sky.

Although slavery ended in Bermuda in 1834, most of the manual labor was done by blacks brought in from the West Indies or seized from the Spanish or Portuguese. A small purple flower found all over the island was named for a former slave. Sally Basset, it was said, was wrongfully accused of trying to poison her master and mistress. After she was burned at the stake, this slender blossom was found among her ashes.

Flies and mosquitoes were a constant annoyance. One sight which Annie and Daniel must have noticed on their travels were the extremely ornate marble gravestones in the island's churchyards which contrasted with the stark white boxes of simple limestone in which Bermudians were buried. They were erected by grieving families who sent the headstones from England to commemorate a loved one lost at sea or in one of the many yellow fever outbreaks.[11] What were Daniel's and Annie's thoughts as they passed these lonely sentinels?

On June 3, once again at sea, the schooner, Clara L. Spark of Provincetown, was sighted. Daniel and one of his mates lowered a boat and rowed over for a visit. This visiting from ship to ship was called "gamming". Often times, members of the crew would also exchange visits during which they would tell stories, sing shanties and, on occasion, dance. Annie who remained on the Tucker notes that "I was abed and sound asleep when they returned." Sounds much like a men's night out. Gamming was a social occasion that was greatly looked forward to by everyone.

June 4 The men caught dolphin fish. "They were so pretty in the water and changed to many colors." Despite their beauty, Annie did not seem upset when they were caught and prepared. "They taste very nice cooked." That same day, she writes, "I saw a large steamer so close that I could see the men on it without my glasses."

June 6 Seven pigeons which had been kept in boxes were set

15

free on deck. One somehow managed to fall overboard. "Poor little thing, he tried so hard to get to the ship that the men lowered a boat and picked him up." They also hauled in a large dolphin fish. "Our little dog, Fido, had a nice time with him after they got him on deck." The wives of whaling captains often brought their dogs with them for company. Birds were also popular because their singing was one of the many things from home which were missed.

June 10 Sanitation was a major problem on all ships with dirt and roaches at the head of the list of concerns. At 6 am, Daniel, disgusted with the lack of cleanliness on his ship, "raided the pantry to see how much dirt he could find." It didn't take long before he discovered "three loaves of moldy bread and mixing pans thick with dough. He told the steward to carry everything on deck, give the pantry a good cleaning and wash all the dishes. By 4 pm, the pantry was finally finished and looked quite neat but how long it will look so is another thing."

One of the less appetizing ways to deal with roaches in food which Annie had to get used to was to tap her bread hard on the table to dislodge the pests. Another approach involved dunking it into her coffee, waiting until the roaches floated to the top and then skimming them off.

June 19 It was a busy day. Annie washed out her laundry. Weather was a main factor in deciding when to launder because the wash was hung on deck to dry. Often, it was necessary to wait for weeks or more in the event it was stormy. When she finished, she cut out two pairs of white duck pants for Daniel She was happy that Mr. Bourne was making her an ironing board. For tea, she unpacked a fruitcake that her mother had made. "It was frosted and trimmed very pretty. The men thought it was almost too pretty to cut but not too pretty to eat after it was cut."

June 25 For the first time, Annie seems sad. It was a long day. "Everything is so quiet. Time does not pass so quickly aboard a whale ship as it does at home. There is no getting ready and going to church, no taking tea with a friend, no interesting meeting to go to in the evening with a pleasant walk home afterward."

Two days later, the uncertainty of life on a whale ship was demonstrated in a dramatic change of events. Annie and Daniel

16

were working together on deck - he was sewing on a boat sail, she, a dress. The soft sounds of the wind in the sails, the clanking of the stays, the splash of the ocean against the side of the ship and the murmur of the men filled the air. Their relaxation and enjoyment of this soft rhythm was suddenly shattered when a shrill cry pierced their calm. "Cooper was jammed by a cask of beef falling on him." Annie reports that he was not seriously hurt.

July 1 It seems as though Annie's mood has not improved. "Another month. I hope for good large whales because the sooner we get the oil, the sooner we start for home."

July 4 Holidays are always a difficult times to be away from loved ones. "I suppose they are having a general holiday at home. Friends will be coming from far and near. I should so enjoy one of mother's good dinners. Not but that we had a good dinner with oyster soup, fresh meat pie and green peas which tasted good though not as fresh as those right out of a garden."

Right after dinner, whales were sighted and the boats were lowered, holiday or no holiday. Unfortunately, not one whale was captured. In observance of the fourth, Daniel and Mr. Bourne sent up some sky rockets which "looked pretty when they came down on the water."

July 5 "I saw a merchant ship from Leghorn (Italy) bound for New York and was pleased that I could send my letter. I think it will be home in a few weeks where I know it will be welcomed."

July 20 Annie was awoken by the cry, "Sperm Whales!" and "was very glad to hear it. All the men had time to eat was a small piece of gingerbread. By 7:30 am, they had lowered three boats. By 3:40 pm, they had returned with a prize, a large sperm whale.

The men looked so tired and hungry but pleased they had a whale. They made it fast alongside the ship where it will lay until morning, when they will commence cutting. Then we'll be in for a greasy time."

After the boats were taken up, dinner was served. (On board ship, dinner was the main meal of the day and was usually served at noon.) "It was late enough for supper but as we had no dinner, I suppose it must be called dinner."

July 21 The weather had become rugged. "It makes it bad for cutting in the whale." The men cut all day. The amount of time necessary for this difficult task depended on the size of the whale - six hours for a small one, twelve for a large. But, in bad weather, it took much longer - five days was customary. Three days was the average amount of time for cutting and boiling out the blubber from a large sperm whale in good weather.

The rough seas prevented the crew from hauling up the head of the whale onto the ship so they attempted to make it fast using chains and ropes but these did not hold. Eventually, much to everyone's frustration, the head and its valuable contents broke away and sank. "We all felt bad. For, it was a large one and would have made a lot of oil. It seemed too bad when the men had worked so hard to try to save it but, of course, we must have the bitter with the sweet."

July 22 "The men are still busy cutting blubber and boiling it. Everyone is covered with grease from the crown of their heads to the soles of their feet. The decks are full of everything and there's not much place to walk. Mr. Bourne, Daniel and I sat on a bench in the evening and watched the iron basket (which held the blubber) burning. There is considerable wind which makes the flames come out all around the basket. It was as pretty as any fireworks I ever saw."

July 23 "Another Sabbath. It doesn't seem much like it with the men boiling out and everything so greasy and dirty." At 9 am, they came upon the whaler, Wave, out of New Bedford, who signaled that there were letters for them. Daniel and Mr. Bourne went aboard and didn't return until after midnight. "They had letters but I had none. I was some disappointed." Annie also noted that the Wave had 80 barrels of oil despite sailing after the Tucker, which, it appears, had less. Just how much less is uncertain.

July 24 The men were still coopering the oil (putting it in barrels). Annie spent the day sewing on a dress she was planning to wear the next time she went on shore. "I have been busy sewing on my 'thin' dress, getting ready to go ashore." She must have been nearing her eighth month and may have found it necessary to increase the size of her clothing. Of course, she would never had discussed her condition in front of the other men. Perhaps, she wondered if they knew. Or, she may have hoped that her wide skirts and shawls covered her secret. Mr. Bourne appears to have been very helpful, during this time.

Although the crew seemed friendly, Annie, most likely, was aware of the many suspicions held by seagoing men - one of the strongest being that a woman onboard brought bad luck. Also that day, "Daniel has finished my birthday present - a bookcase. It is a real beauty." (Actually, Annie turned thirty on July 14, so Daniel's gift was a bit late, which she doesn't mention just as she fails to tell us what she did to celebrate the occasion)

July 25 The oil was still being stowed away. Annie was afraid that someone would get hurt lugging the heavy barrels below deck. "And, they have to holler so, it is enough to frighten anyone."

July 28 "It seems to be the same thing over and over again aboard a whale ship. Unless we get a whale or speak (meet and talk to) a vessel, we have no news to write."

August 4 "Squally and rugged. Daniel has been down in the cabin painting it white which will make it a great deal lighter. He has stuffed one of the chairs and I guess the room will look real nice when he gets done. I have been making bowties for him to wear ashore."

August 8 At 6:30 am, large sperm whales were sighted. The men immediately set off. When they returned at 5 pm, they didn't get one. If they had, Annie wrote, "they would have done a good season's work. I was real disappointed."

August 14 Daniel and Annie took advantage of the warm weather to do their laundry. Once that was finished, Annie kept busy sewing and reading. She was delighted that Daniel had begun to make a writing desk out of mahogany for her. "He worked on it most of the day."

August 20 Mr. Bourne caught a turtle and Annie had some of it made into soup for dinner. "It was real nice and tasted like chicken soup. For tea, we had some of the liver and meat fried. It was just as tender as could be and the first I ever ate."

The next good day, Annie had all of their bedding and clothing brought up on deck to air. What with Daniel's painting their quarters and making furniture and Annie's sewing and airing their things, it probably should have been suspected that there was a reason. If her condition had been known, it would have been perfectly obvious that they both were following the age old custom of nesting - preparing for the birth of their child. How excited they must have been! Perhaps, along with the

19

anticipation, they may have felt some apprehension that such an important occasion may have to take place in the middle of an ocean.

Chapter 4

By the last week in August, after three months at sea, they had reached Corbo Island in the Azores. As they approached, Annie stood on the deck and looked out over the harbor at the town of Fayal where they were hoping to land. Clustered near the harbor were the docks and beyond them, small houses and other buildings. Some were left natural and showed the native stone of which they were built, others were whitewashed. The contrast between the two was pleasing. The town was surrounded by very high mountains. Most of the town's 1600 inhabitants were a mix of Portuguese and African.

August 23 "Their roofs are made very strangely. They call it tileing them instead of shingling as we have at home. They look very clumsy and the pieces are shaped like our stove pipe would look if sawed lengthwise and then cut in small pieces and one piece layed above the other. I could see the church and three to four windmills where they grind their corn. It is very mountainous. I would like to go ashore but it is very rugged and a bad place to land. I would have to jump from rock to rock and with the water rushing up on them, it was very slippery. It was no place for a lady to land."

Annie watched as Daniel and Mr. Vanderhoop, the third mate, took a boat and crew and went ashore. It must have been difficult for her to be left on board, at that stage in her pregnancy. She must have been very concerned about getting to land in time for the birth of her baby. What would have happened if her time came and Daniel were not there to help? The thought of giving birth alone with only Mr. Bourne and a ship full of men must have been unbearable. But nothing is written in her journal about her feelings at this time.

Later that day Daniel returned. "I didn't expect him. It was so rugged. The governor's wife sent me a dozen apples, white grapes, and a sprig of lavender which made me think of home. The apples tasted nice as I had not had any such thing for a long time. He also brought back beef and green corn but the corn was too old to eat."

The next day, more than two dozen natives rowed their boats through the rough water out to the ship to deliver the other provisions Daniel had ordered while he was in port. Even though Annie was in their quarters below deck, she could hear their chatter as they transferred the beets, potatoes, pumpkins, onions, chickens, eggs and watermelons from their boats to the ship. "I never heard such a noisy tribe, they acted as though they were crazy. Among them were two little boys who brought a bag with two bunches of white grapes and three apples. They came to my room and gave them to me with a large musk melon. They came at noon and left at one. I was glad to see the last of them. My husband traded for fruit of all kinds and some milk so I had a feast for a few days."

Another day of very bad weather. "I have had to lay abed most of the day. At dinner, the vessel gave a roll and away went my cup of tea in my lap and the victuals went in every direction! Of course, I had to make a hearty laugh. I have tried sitting on my trunk and on a box and on the floor but find one place as good as another for the ship will pitch and roll in spite of everything. Daniel says it's as bad a sea as he ever saw for it seems to be all in heaps going every which way. I think I am getting to be quite a sailor for I have not been sick at all."

August 26 Although the weather was still rough, Annie accompanied Daniel to shore. There were many men and women on the landing. Daniel proceeded ahead in order to give his papers to the doctor who was standing at the end of the pier. He wanted to know the name of their vessel, where it was from, how much whale oil it contained, what ports it had been to and if there was any sickness among the passengers. As Annie was climbing the twenty or so steps to the dock, a heavy breaker completely covered her. "Daniel and a gentleman hauled me up. I was very frightened and weak."

Dazed and wet to the skin, she was hardly able to walk to the hotel where they would be staying. At first, she found it very gloomy. "When I went in the long entry with its stone floor and walls and its long heavy door to the head of the stairs, we had to unlock the door before we could enter. All I could think of was prison."

But, once inside, "it was much pleasanter. The hotel keeperand his wife were English. In the parlor I met a lady from NewYork.Soon, Mr. Bourne brought a good package of lettersfromhome which I prized highly. We dined at 2 pm on soup, fowl, meats of different kinds and fruits. We had a nice room on the first floor looking out on the harbor." After dinner, she lay down and read the letters and then, up once again, dressed for tea at 7 pm.

Not long after their arrival, Annie made an entry into her journal that gives some hint of her pregnancy. She and Daniel had met Captain and Mrs. Tabor and their daughter from Fairhaven, Massachusetts. They happened to be staying at the same hotel. "I was overcome when I met her. She was in a very trying condition as well as myself and was feeling bad that her husband was not going to stop ashore with her." The fact that Annie records that she was "overcome" when she met Mrs. Tabor and that she found her "in a very trying condition as well as myself" provides a touching indication of her feelings at that time but there is little more on this subject. She and Mrs. Tabor had tea in the parlor where their husbands joined them after they had had their smoke. According to Annie, they had a "pleasant chat." She notes that when she and Daniel returned to their room, she was tired but opened a box from home which was "filled with nice things. I have got such a kind mother and father to think of me when I am so far away from them." Annie began to feel badly and Daniel offered to put her items back in the box for her.

August 29 "I had a poor night's rest and cannot get up. Daniel called for the doctor. About 9:26 am, our little girl was born. I am very proud of it. A lady, Mrs. Graham, who was stopping at the hotel, came in and dressed the baby. She stayed all night which was very kind of her for Daniel was very tired."

August 30 "I was very proud and happy when I awoke to see our baby lying on my arm. My husband went to breakfast where they treated and congratulated him. After he returned, Daniel couldn't stay away from our baby. He carried it around the room as proud as a father could be. A nurse came, a Portuguese woman, but I could not make her understand much of anything." How frustrating that must have been for a new mother not to be able to communicate with the very person who could most help her.

"All at the hotel think my baby is very pretty. Of course, we do too. Such a tiny thing, she only weighed three pounds." Was Annie not a bit concerned over this small size? The attention of the guests must have warmed them and ease their fears about the

23

baby's size. But, in that hotel room, surrounded by the many well -wishers, Annie must have felt the need for her own family, especially her mother. She was so far from home.

August 31 The baby was very sick. "She cried out with pain all day and towards night, I noticed that her cry was weaker. When Daniel came in, I will never forget how he looked at me. Our baby only breathed two more times. It did not seem to me that I could ever give her up. They took her away from me to put in the next room. Daniel found some little clothes with narrow pink ribbon to lay her out. He tied it around the waist and its sleeves. They bought her in and she looked just as though she was asleep. She looked too nice to lay away in the ground."

September 1 "We had the baby's picture taken. Daniel had to pay $5 but I do not begrudge the money because that picture is all that I can ever have of my little one. She was put in the coffin, a little white casket. They do not make their coffins here as they do at home but it was a pretty one, the nicest we could get. After noon, a hack came. Daniel and his friends, Consul Dabney and Captain Burke, went to the grave. Our baby was layed in a green spot with trees to shade it. Now that my little one is an angel in heaven, she is much better off than she would be in this wicked world of ours. I must try to be reconciled because I know that Jesus has her safe with him."

For many days, there is no entry in the journal. It must have been a monumental effort for Annie to reconcile the loss of her baby, to know that the memories of their child would be so brief. That they would have little to share with their family and friends. That their little one would never see the sky, the sun, her grandparents. That what they had waited for with such anticipation was gone forever.

September 12 Mrs. Tabor came to call. Later, she delivered "another daughter, a fine baby, weighing seven pounds." A week, later, Annie writes: "The Tabor baby died. Its death brought up everything that was so fresh about my little one. It is hard for us." She went to see Mrs. Tabor although she became very tired after taking only a few steps. "I am not very strong, yet."

September 26 "Daniel ordered a hack and we went for a ride. I don't know when I have enjoyed anything as I did that ride."

Except for her visit to Mrs. Tabor, Annie had been confined for close to one month. Perhaps, she felt it was time to get out, to try to rediscover some pleasure in life.

October 3, The A.R. Tucker returned to port, two weeks earlier than expected. Mr. Bourne had taken the ship out in search of whales but without success. Daniel wanted to leave the Azores. He must have worried about the amount of oil they had gotten on their voyage, so far. And, it was risky for the men to be in port - there were too many temptations - liquor, women and desertion. While they were anchored at Fayal, Mr. Bourne noted in his log that five men had jumped overboard and tried to swim to shore. One of them was captured but the others got away. Or, more than likely, they drowned because they were almost a mile out and there was a strong tide.

"I had gotten stronger and Daniel was anxious to be on the way. Mr. Bourne and I went shopping. It was fun trying to make them understand what we wanted and making change."

October 5 "We had accumulated quite a number of things. It was difficult packing." Once they were on ship, they "went up on the stern to see our friends up on the hill. I waved my handkerchief and they returned my wave. It would be a long time before I would have the pleasure of women's society, again, but I am content to have Daniel's."

Daniel's concerns about getting underway were justified, the next day, when cooper jumped overboard and tried to swim to shore. They were four miles out. As soon as he was spotted, a boat was lowered to pick him up. It was soon discovered that he had been drinking, having gotten some liquor from the shore boat.

Annie, throughout her journal, shows the high regard she held for her husband but one cannot but wonder if she may have been puzzled by the frequent attempts to desert. These men were obviously risking their lives to get to land. Was it just because a life at sea was not what they wanted? One missionary, Luther Gulick, called the whaling ship "the most disgusting of moral pesthouses." Often they were overcrowded, dirty and filled with discontented and bored men. Because the crewmembers were not paid a wage but rather a share in the ship's profits, a lay, many actually ended up in debt to the vessel's owners and were forced to ship out, once again.

25

Or was there something more? Had these deserters been forcibly removed from their homeland and brought to the ship? Impressment was common, at that time. In many cases, unsuspecting men were stunned by the affects of drugs or drink and brought aboard a ship. Mr. Bourne does say in his log that he "brought off four Portuguese and took them on board." Whether this was done with their consent, there is no way of knowing.

October 8, "We saw the General Scott with Captain and Mrs. Tabor on board but it was too rough for me to visit." Annie must have been very disappointed not to see Mrs. Tabor with whom she had shared so much. Daniel did make it over to their ship and exchanged gifts, including papers, books and a straw hat Annie sent for Captain Tabor. Daniel returned with four cans of condensed milk.

Chapter 5

After several days sailing the Atlantic, the Tucker arrived at the island of Teneriffe. This is the largest of the seven major Canary Islands located just off the northwest coast of Africa. The name of these islands has nothing to do with a tiny bird but rather comes from the large dogs (canes) who were originally found living, there. Teneriffe, which means white mountain, is believed by some natives to be one of the upper peaks of Atlantis, the continent that sank into the ocean, many years ago. It is an island of extremes - very dry on its southern end and, in the north, humid and green.

Annie was excited to be going ashore. She was "lowered over the side of the boat in the chair that Mr. Bourne and the cooper made." After reaching their hotel, "I sat in the parlor with a New Yorker and had ice-cream. In a Spanish place like this, ladies do not go out much until evening. Then they dress up and promenade with their long dresses trailing the ground. Ladies and gentlemen do not walk together." Later, when they did go out, "a band began playing from 8 until 10 pm. We left before they were finished because we were so tired." As they were returning to their hotel, a man-of-war came into the harbor and fired a twenty-one gun salute.

October 13 "We went to visit the home of Consul Dabney and his family which was located about six miles out of town. On the way, I saw cochineal plants (host plants to insects used to produce red dye). We passed three camels with packs on their backs going along as deliberate as you please." At the Dabneys, "we had a lunch of white bread, butter, preserves, pears, apricots, figs, cheese and wine." Afterwards, Annie retired to the room of Mrs. Dabney who was an invalid. One of the daughters played and sang. On a walk in the garden, she saw the men gathering cochineal plants. They "use a brush to keep the bugs off, clean and cut the leaves and lay them on the ground so to enrich it." At dinner, "in came a man servant with soup, fish, potatoes, mutton stew, pudding, and fruit. Afterwards, the youngest daughter played and sang some amusing pieces. One of these was called 'Way Down in Maine'. Both daughters danced in the Spanish style. They used castanets, making considerable noise. The youngest daughter showed chessmen she'd been carving

27

beautifully." When Daniel and Annie returned to their hotel, they both went, once again, for ice-cream which, not being available onboard ship, must have been a real treat.

The next day, the same New Yorker they had met on arrival "hired seats for a concert. I forgot to carry my fan ashore and every lady carries one. If she doesn't, she attracts attention. So the New Yorker borrowed the landlady's fan for me. The music was very good. Daniel sent for ice-cream but it was frozen water with peppermint and I didn't like it."

Before leaving Teneriffe, they took on some Portuguese crew to replace the men they lost in Fayal. They also bought supplies including, according to Mr. Bourne's log, 4700 gallons of fresh water. On October 29, black fish were sighted and the boats were lowered for them but did not get far. It was the first time that anything had been seen to lower a boat for since August 13, notes Mr. Bourne in the ship's log.

During this time, Annie kept herself busy reading, writing letters and her journal and working on a chair seat. She "broke out" her sewing supplies to see if the material was damp. "It looked nice - the white cloth and calico." She napped a lot and played some music on her pipe organ. Daniel had the men paint the boat. "The men seem to be always busy."

It was Annie's first Thanksgiving on the Tucker. "We had boiled chicken and all the fixings including peach pudding. We almost lost Mr. Bourne who was under the jib boom when the ship suddenly plunged." But, it all turned out well in the end, thankfully.

"We have now gone around the Cape of Good Hope," Annie writes. The cape is a rocky headland on the Atlantic coast of South Africa. It was of special significance to sailors as a major milestone on the routes followed by ships to the Far East and Australia. An area of rugged wildness, it has fostered many legends including that of *The Flying Dutchman* whose crew was doomed to sail the surrounding waters without ever rounding the cape. The mythic character, Adamastor, in the epic poem, *Os Lusiadas,* which was first printed in 1572, was a symbol of the natural dangers Portuguese navigators faced trying to go around the cape.

The Tucker's journey past that famous landmark appears to have been uneventful because all Annie says about it is, "Daniel says it will be all sliding down the hill now because we are more apt to have fair winds and plenty of whales."

December 3 "Cold and cheerless. I would like to be home but since I cannot, I will write in my journal. I 'met' a Dutch captain traveling on the Batavia which was loaded with coal. I got very much interested in talking with the flags and picking out the answers in a book we have. I was able to carry on a conversation as if we were in the same parlor even though we were miles apart."

There was much excitement when an albatross was captured. Of flying birds, the albatross is considered to be one of the largest. The one Annie saw had "wings across measuring 10 feet four inches from tip to tip."

The weather was bad for the next several days.

December 13 "Very unpleasant day. It rained all day and there was a very heavy sea. There were leaks all over the ship. Our stateroom was wet, most all over. At dinner, the ship gave a roll and over went the tureen of bean soup, stewed pumpkin and boiled onions onto the floor. It was a very laughable affair."

December 14 "Still tossing and rolling about. I went up to the head of the stairs and there was blowing such a sea as I never saw before. It looked just as though it was angry and didn't know what to do with itself. Everything is damp. The water is dropping all over the cabin where the deck leaks, above. This is the third day of bad weather and I have to stay below. The days seem very long when I cannot get on deck."

At long last the weather broke.

December 23 "Near St. Paul Island in the southernmost Indian Ocean." This volcanic island is located halfway between South Africa and Australia. It is one of the most isolated in the world. "It is so nice and warm. I took my work and book on deck. Later, Daniel took me sailing. We sailed close to an island and I could see the wreck of an English iron steamer. We decided to go ashore. As we neared the wharf, I threw my little dog, Fido, into the water and let him swim the short distance. He hadn't been ashore since we left home and seemed very pleased. There were still materials on shore from the wreck. There were mahogany chairs and other provisions. I sat in one of my new chairs with a flag thrown over it."

December 25 "It is Christmas. The last one, Daniel and I

were at home and we enjoyed ourselves very much." Annie writes nothing else about what she did, that day, or on the first day of the new year.

Her first entry for 1872 was about more bad weather.

January 8 "It was quite a blow. I have had a chair put up in the bed and pillows fixed up so I can sit and sew. All day long, I have heard men falling on the deck, above."

January 12 "Calm. It is so nice on deck after staying below for five and a half days. Daniel is taking down the sink in our room and making a place for the wash bowl, pitcher and tumblers in the small room. It is going to make my room a good large room having the sink away. Mr. Bourne is making a door between the two rooms that will slide. I have been changing the dirt in my hanging plants and washing the dust off their leaves. The bird got out of her cage while I was fixing it but I caught it."

While Daniel and Mr. Bourne were working on her room, Annie saw something in the water that looked very strange. It was a fine red substance that floated on the surface. She called Daniel to see if he knew what it was. "Daniel tells me it is called brill, little shelled creatures that the right whale scoops up in its mouth."

January 23 "We have had all kinds of weather - pleasant then a squall with thunder and lightning. It's hard to find a place to sit without getting wet."

January 27 "We have reached the Island of Bouton, Celebes," located between the Indian and Pacific Oceans and halfway between the Philippines and Australia. The inhabitants of this tropical paradise were basically Malay and Polynesian. Most were Muslims. Today, the Malay Archipelago, of which it is a part, is known as Indonesia.

"Daniel said that we could go ashore, if the natives were friendly." It was well known what could happen in the case of unfriendly natives. Whole crews had been wiped out. An added danger was cannibalism. Not that the natives were totally to blame. Some unscrupulous ship captains kidnapped them and made them members of their crews. They tore them away from their families and forced them to work on their ships. Many died. For this reason, the natives had learned to distrust and fear foreigners.

Mr. Bourne and Mr. Vanderloop went on ahead. "When we got towards land, we saw them shaking hands with the natives, some dozen of them with knives and spears." Daniel needed fire wood so he and the men jumped out of our shore boat into the water and waded to shore. "I had to wait for the tide so the boat could go up to the beach. While waiting I looked over the side of the boat and saw beautiful pieces of coral and shells on the bottom." Mr. Bourne carried Annie over the wet sand.

The old chief invited them to his hut. "To get in, we had to step on poles put across like bars, a good way apart. They spread a long mat down for me to sit on. It was made of rattan. The hut, of bamboo. He cut a coconut for us to drink the milk. There were several native women and little babies, there. The chief sent after his wives who seemed not to live in the hut we were in. Seven or eight came. All had on large hats and some calico sewed together and put on one shoulder and down on the other hip. Some did not wear any. They wore a calico shirt. The men wear nothing but a small piece of cloth round them. The chief and his son wear considerable clothing of bright red cloth. The babies don't wear any."

They did not stop long. "I didn't see anything attractive. Daniel traded an old musket for chickens. I had the gun powder in my pocket so I took it out and gave it to the chief. He bowed and kissed his hand to me. The men traded cotton and red cloth for twenty-three chickens, bananas, sugar cane, different kinds of fish and something that looked very much like a lobster in shape. I put it in rum to try to save it," (when they returned to the ship.)

31

Chapter 6

Once again, they were at sea when an incident occurred which took them all by surprise. Annie was watching the men at their work when she noticed Andrew Loo, one of the South Sea Islanders, whom she called by the term kanaka, talking to the ship keeper. When they finished their conversation, Andrew began climbing aloft. He had just reached his perch above, when, without warning, he plunged down. "He struck his head on an iron rail and was killed instantly. He went down into the water like a log, before the men could lower the boat. We had been alerted by the cry of another kanaka. There were three of them who came from Tahiti. They had been together for many years whaling. His death cast a gloom over the whole ship, having one of their number taken away without any warning. I was much frightened and can think of nothing else."

Well into February, they reached Ternate in the Molucca Sea in the Pacific Ocean which, today, is part of eastern Indonesia. This heavily forested, volcanic island was known for its aromatic spices. "We visited with Captain and Mrs. Brown and Captain and Mrs. Edwards at the Edwards house. It was all on one floor. The rooms were very large and airy with a large piazza in front where we sat most of the time. The food is different from home but some of the dishes are very nice." After weeks at sea in the company of only men, it must have been a welcome respite for Annie to be with other women and to share their company and conversation.

February 19 "After dinner, we went to a place called China Camp where there was music and dancing and a procession. It was the king's birthday. I had noticed when we were coming into the harbor that all the vessels at anchor had a good display of bunting. The streets were full of people. The children were having a fine time firing off fire crackers.

Captain Edwards asked us to go into one of the Chinese houses. We were received very kindly and were offered tea out of little tiny cups and saucers and other refreshments. The house was very pretty with some attractive ornaments. The only way I could talk with them was through Captain Edwards as they speak Malay. In the street, the dancers were dressed with tall paper caps and masks and their pants and coats were all covered with little strips of paper which made a soft rustling noise when they were dancing. Only the men participated but some of them dressed in women's dresses."

February 20 "They killed a bullock for a sacrifice at one of the churches. After dinner, Daniel proposed a walk so we started out to a Mahomet (Muslim) village where we saw two Mahomet churches. (Ternate was one of the earliest places in the region to which Islam spread, probably coming from Java in the late fifteenth century. In the beginning, the faith was restricted to Ternate's small ruling family but spread slowly to the rest of the population.) They let us go up the steps and look in but not to step over the door sill.

Some of the people were at worship. They sat on rattan mats, saying something over and over, all together. There was a crowd in the churchyard, around the bullock that had been killed.

At the other church, we saw a boy worshipping on the veranda. He knelt on a mat and kept putting his head down on the floor and crossing himself. He seemed very sincere for he did not notice us. When he finished his devotions, he was surprised to see us there."

The village consisted of one street with a soldiers' barrack at its head. Annie, Daniel and their friends passed on to a large green level space of about thirty acres which led up to a hill on which stood a beautiful large house belonging to the sultan. "He never goes out because his feet trouble him. He has a wife but she is never seen by anyone. It is a rare thing for him to receive visitors and his house is guarded by soldiers. Daniel had visited him years ago. He says he has a high throne he sits on with a great number of cushions."

That night, they returned to their Chinese hosts at the China Camp for more festivities including music, dancing and a procession. They had "a horse made out of wire and covered with a very thin cloth and a light inside so it would show through. It was on wheels with a little boy riding on its back. There was a large deer, made out of wood and painted, which was very natural, with a boy riding on it. There was a carriage with two seats which held six children. They were dressed up with all kinds of things that would sparkle and shine. Chinese lanterns hung on top of the carriage which was drawn by natives. Some of the men were in strange dress and had masks on."

"At the Chinaman's, we met a number of the first people of the place. They dressed very much like our people at home. Some of the young ladies and gentlemen waltzed. The room was large and airy and nice for dancing. Servants passed round the tea and coffee and wines and cakes and sweetmeats and cigars to the gentlemen, all evening."

The day they went to sea, they met Captain Brown's ship, the Benjamin Cummings, and visited. "Mrs. Brown has beautiful accommodations. Their ship is large which makes her large rooms below. I enjoyed it very much going aboard."

March 10 "We saw the Benjamin Cummings. Daniel invited the Browns aboard. She waved her handkerchief and I returned the salute by waving mine. They brought us a piece of fresh pork and a book. I played on the organ and talked."

March 13 "I saw the island of Kabruang, (still Indonesia) this morning. I thought we would be in Salibaboo but about 10 am, I heard the cry, 'There she blows!' Daniel had been breaking out dishes for trade and had just found my checkerboard which I thought was lost. He quickly went aloft. They were sperm whales. The boats were lowered as soon as they could get ready, about 11 am. At 4 pm the men returned. Mr. Bourne with a small whale, Mr. Vanderloop with a larger one. Mr. Harris didn't get any.

March 15 This morning, I watched the blubber boiling. Mr. Bourne took hold of my hand or I should fall down for the decks were all covered with grease. I had my rubbers on, too. One of the pots was full of oil boiling, the other full of scraps. They had a large skimmer to skim the scraps out with. The mincing machine cut the pieces of whale in slices, still not cutting them way through but leaving it hanging together in one long piece. The men turned over the pieces in the pot with a long two tine fork."

It took several days to cut in and store the oil. Just as it was finished, the Tucker dropped anchor at Salibaboo. They were still in the South Pacific. Immediately, the decks were filled with natives who were interested in trading. That evening, as they waited to go ashore the next day, Mr. King and Mr. Lawrence, mates from the Stafford, came to visit. "I got out my albums and stereoscope views and backgammon board. They seemed to enjoy looking at them very much and did not take

Annie Holmes Ricketson, from the archives of
The New Bedford Whaling Museum

*Captain Daniel Ricketson, from the archives of
The New Bedford Whaling Museum*

The bark, A. R. Tucker, *from the archives of*
The New Bedford Whaling Museum

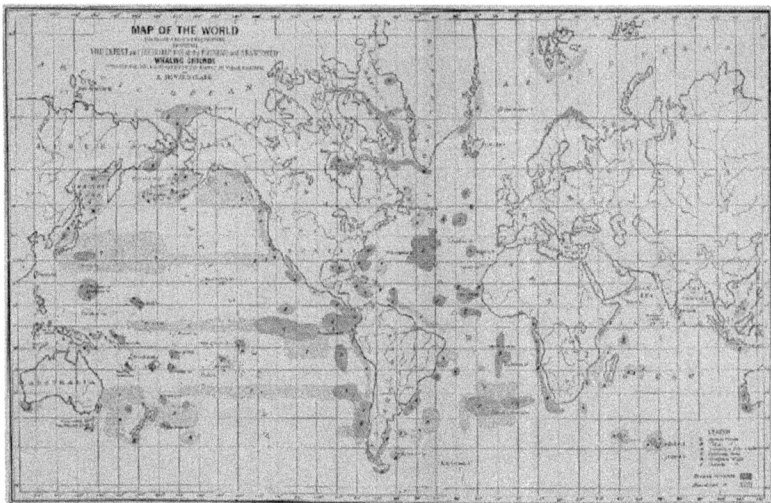

Map of the world whaling grounds, 1860, credit to the National Oceanic and Atmospheric Administration/Deparmtment of Commerce

their leave until 10:30 pm."

March 19 "In all of these places, they have what they call a king, some places have two.

They have two in Salibaboo. We went to one of the king's houses. It had nice steps in front compared to other places. The house was quite grand, the room we went into was large, some 45 feet square. In the center was a big table made of black ebony with setees of the same material on each side and also an armchair. All were roughly made. Daniel took the armchair at the head of the table. I sat on one of the setees opposite the king, his wife and mother and father.

They ate beetle nut and Daniel had a smoke. They broke a coconut for me. At one end of the room sat a woman making cloth, at the other was a fire where they cooked. They had strange looking cooking utensils. No stove but rather four pieces of round iron the same as the bottom of a kettle. Between these, they make a fire and set kettles over them. There is no chimney and the smoke came right out in the room. Two hundred people lived there. The men and women wear clothes, the children do not."

Annie had just returned to the ship, when the other king and his wife came to visit. "I had to entertain them as best as I could. I played on the organ. It was amusing to see them stare at it to see where the sound came from. I showed them my stereoscope views which were a great wonder to them."

The queen brought many gifts including three baskets each filled with beans and potatoes, a beautiful bird and three round baskets made on one of the islands. "When they bring a present, they expect one in return. If you do not give them something, they will ask. I gave her several little presents that amounted in value to as much as she brought me."

Daniel and Annie paid another visit to the Browns onboard their ship. Mrs. Brown and Annie worked on their sewing. "Mrs. Brown is tucking me a skirt on the sewing machine while I work on a pattern of a butterfly on a tidy. It was amusing to see the natives shake their heads at the sewing machine. I imagine it was the wonderfullest thing they ever saw. One morning, Captain Brown insisted on finishing the work on my skirt. He sews more than Mrs. Brown on the machine."

After dinner, they went with the Browns to visit both of the kings. At the first house, they tried to communicate with the queen only to discover that she was totally deaf. But when they went to the other king, his family got out their music and danced. "Their instruments were strange and included bamboo sticks, a great brass gong and several little drums. It was the strangest dance I ever saw. They never smile and hardly move their feet but keep their hands going with the music and move their body a very little. The men played music and danced first, then the girls. Then they sang. They cut coconuts to drink which we did justice to as we were very dry. There was a heavy shower and when it cleared, we started for the ship."

Annie and her husband went ashore to the king's house for more music and dancing. "It is their custom to take a handkerchief in one hand and a fan in the other when dancing and when through, they put the handkerchief in some one's lap and that one is expected to dance. One of them put it in my lap so I got up and I did the best that I could. We had a very amusing time."

By the first of April, they were back at sea searching for whales. One day, they stopped at Louisa Island, not too far from Salibaboo, to trade with the natives. Annie bought coconut oil for her hair which had become dry and sugar cane to sweeten their food and drink.

For the next few days, Daniel was kept busy caring for several members of the crew including the cook who had fallen ill. When he went down to steerage, he found them in great distress and gave them some medicine. During the night, Daniel was up several times taking care of the sick men. He became all tired out. "I have done nothing. The ship is going so fast that I do not feel well at all," Annie writes.

April 6 "The sun is so hot that I fear sun stroke. The men are making an awning for shade. We spend our evenings playing backgammon. Mr. Bourne is showing us how as neither of us know how to play." Captain Moulton sent over a nice bottle of wine. "He also sent over a watch case to take its pattern. It having a free mason design upon it, my husband is anxious to have one made. (Daniel was a member of the Free and Accepted Masons.) I have been laying down most of the day, the weather being so warm, it takes all my strength."

April 11 "Just before dinner, the lookout cried out 'white water' but I did not see anything more until 1 pm. They raised whales and at quarter to 2, they lowered four boats. At 4 pm, Daniel returned with a whale that he got and one that Mr. Bourne got. Mr. Harris got the third whale. At 5 pm, all hands were on deck and the boats back on their cranes with three whales alongside.

Toby, a Kanaka, was lost during the hunt. A whale struck him and knocked him overboard instantly. He sank right down beside the whale's head. The men thought that he was going right into the whale's mouth. It was good luck getting the whales, but the sad news took away all the pleasure."

The Ricketsons visited the Stafford. The second mate, Mr. Lawrence, gave Annie a card with reading upon it (postcard) to put in her album.

April 15 "We were disappointed especially when we found out that there had been a good opportunity to catch a whale which had been lost by a careless throw by the boat steerer, named Allen. Daniel is going to have him go in his boat the next time."

April 18 "My husband got a man from the Stafford by the name of Thomas. Loosing Toby, a boat steerer, and another one being sick made us short. We let the Captain have a Portuguese, Anthorne." Neither of these men appeared to have a choice in this exchange.

April 24 While steering the ship, "Mr. Bourne struck a porpoise and got him. They generally sink but this one floated and so they lowered a boat and picked him up. Of course, we had porpoise balls and cakes for tea."

April 28 "We visited a merchant vessel and met a very pleasant English lady and her husband. They were bound to Sidney on the bark, the Novelty. They had a splendid, great cabin all fitted out for taking passengers. The decks were very roomy. There were only nine persons aboard besides the captain and his wife. She gave me a bundle of papers and seven bound books, a can of blueberries, a jar of preserved ginger, and a half dozen eggs. The captain gave me a pretty present, something that an insect made beneath the water, which I prize very highly." (an amber)

Chapter 7

It was May 2. Annie had been away from home exactly one year and was having a difficult time. "I recall the sad day a year ago when I left mother and father and a pleasant home to make my home upon the restless ocean. I seem to hear my mother's cry when I took her parting kiss and to see my father as he stood on the wharf watching the pilot boat bearing me away from him. It was a sad day to them as well as to me. I know they feel lonely and miss me very much as I do them. What a happy, happy day it will be if we all live to meet again."

There is no way of knowing how Annie handled her feelings of sadness and separation because she rarely mentions them. But, most likely, she kept herself busy. For two weeks, there is nothing recorded in her journal.

On the afternoon of May 15, whales were, once again, sighted from the masthead. There had not been one sighting since April 11, when they were able to capture two whales. All four boats were lowered. Annie watched as her husband and his officers boarded the boats and set off. When they returned in the darkness, not one whale had been captured. "I feel sorry for we had not seen whales for so long a time," Annie wrote.

When they met up with the Stafford, in June, Captain Moulton came aboard and brought with him a bundle of newspapers. At sea, this type of delivery was the only way to keep up with the news. As soon as she could, Annie read each and every item, even those articles which she would have ordinarily skipped over. Also, she was impressed to learn that "Captain Moulton and his crew had taken fifty barrels of oil since we saw them last."

June 18 "Exciting times. We struck and got four porpoises. Then we set the try works to going and tryed out the porpoises ending with a half a barrel of oil." (Porpoises are small cetaceans and are related to whales and dolphins. They are distinct from dolphins.)

On June 19, Captain Howland of the Kathleen came to visit. "We had a pleasant time. He was acquainted with some of the folk at home that we knew." A few days later, whales were sighted but after all four boats were lowered, they lost them.

July 7 "We went over to Leron, (either near or on the island of Salibaboo) some seven miles from the ship and stayed all day. For dinner we had rice balls which I think were made from coconut oil, boiled sweet potatoes, fish fried some way with a gravy. Chicken was served the same way but everything was seasoned up so high with red peppers that I could hardly eat it. We ate at a round table with legs but only an inch high. We had to sit on the floor and take the plates in our laps. We had large spoons to eat with, that they got aboard some ship. One man's wife was only fourteen years. She had been married three years and had one child. I invited them aboard our ship as his wife had never been aboard a ship."

The next day they "again went ashore to where they get water for the ship. It was a very pretty place. We went back to the ship for dinner and then we went over to a small island opposite Leron. It has no name on the chart but is a lovely little island with a beautiful sand beach. We carried clothes to go in bathing. We went in and had a nice bathe. After, Daniel went off gunning and I went along the beach picking up shells."

July 10 We "went to Mowang which is half the way to Salibaboo." (According to a 2002 survey by the National Institute of Aeronautics and Space, Indonesia has 18,306 islands. Counting tidal islands, which are periodically submerged, doubles the figure and many islands with no name or the same names, make if very confusing even to the government of Indonesia.) "We met Captain Mouton and went to the king's house which was made nicer than any we have been into yet. All the post and beams were black ebony and the place was layed out better. A schoolmaster took us to the schoolhouse which was a large building with only one room with a chair and a table for the schoolmaster and benches round the side for the children. They had books and slates and a large smooth board for a black board. The schoolmaster gave me a book. It was a Malay singing book."

July 20 "We went into Ternate. (Ternate is the island they visited where they went to China Town and the Muslim village and churches.) Captain Edwards and his family were well. There were seven letters for us with some papers. The sad news was the death of my aunt and that father had been dangerously sick but was better in the last letter. Of course, I did not sleep much that night." Annie's great distance from her family and loved ones must have weighed heavily on her mind.

August 2 "We hurried back to the ship. A squall was coming and I was afraid I might get wet. Later, we exchanged books and papers with Captain Forman of the Adeline Gibbs."

August 9 "We visited with Captain and Mrs. Lavers of the Sunbeam. The first mate, Mr. Clark, gave me a new dress. The captain sent over two boxes of shoes to see if any fit. I took two pair and Mrs. Lavers sent me some papers."

August 17 "I saw several barks. We got so close to one that I could see the men on deck, very plain. There was a large dog and I heard him bark."

August 18 "There was a heavy squall. Daniel and Mr. Bourne both went up on deck. It blowed away the fore top mast sail. It went with a bang! Steward and cook killed a hog and we had roast spare rib for dinner. We had just sat down when the ship gave a pitch and over went the dish of gravy and everything on the table gave a jump."

After many days of squalls, September 7 was a beautiful, calm day. "We are anxious to get to the whaling grounds. I spent the day embroidering and putting braid on one of my dresses." They had had no oil since they struck the four porpoises on June 18.

October 1 "Daniel and I washed. The men are making rope and working in the rigging. The islands of Matthias and New Hanover are in sight."

October 3 "We traded coconuts with natives from New Hanover (a volcanic island in the Bismarck Archipelago of Papua New Guinea, PNG). They came out in canoes." It is estimated that more than a thousand different cultural groups have existed in PNG. Because of this diversity, many different styles of cultural expression have emerged. Each group has created its own art, dance, weaponry, costumes, singing, music, and building design. Most of these different groups have their own language. Those who become skilled at hunting, farming and fishing are highly respected.

"Daniel got up in the stern and traded. He gave a piece of iron hoop about a finger long for three or four coconuts. While trading, there was a cry from aloft. 'There she blows.' Daniel dropped the iron hoop, jumped into the rigging and went aloft. The natives were frightened. They didn't know what it all meant. They left."

All four boats were lowered for the hunt. There was much excitement but the men were not able to get near before their prey sounded and disappeared beneath the sea.

While Daniel and the crew were out after the whales, the natives returned. "They do not wear any clothes, at all. They are powerful looking, strong built but my husband has said he thinks that they are a weak set."

This time, when the natives returned, there were "twelve to twenty canoes with coconuts and bananas. They wanted to trade but the shipkeeper was in fear. There were so many of them and they were so hard looking. We had only five men left aboard so he came down from aloft and tried to keep them from coming alongside. He took a gun and pointed it at them (it was not loaded) and one of them jumped into the water. But the shipkeeper couldn't get them to go and more canoes were coming so he hoisted the colors for the boats to return. After that, they did not trouble us and eventually left."

"Some of them had their hair, wool I should have said, colored red and some, white. One man had some black stuff put all over his face in streaks. Cook had got three kettles of boiling water ready just in case. Daniel and his crew returned without a whale. I felt so bad for them. They had worked so hard and got nothing."

October 5 "I fired a pistol. It was my first attempt." After Annie had been left with only a crew of five to protect the ship from unruly natives, Daniel must have decided that this unusual action was necessary for her own protection. Mr. Bourne recorded in his log that the natives that they were encountering were armed with bows and arrows. He made several entries about the "great many canoes about the ship."

October 17 "While Daniel was ashore, the natives came back. Mr. Bourne would not let them over the rail but their heads kept coming up so that I could see them and, of all that I ever set my eyes on, they were the worse. They had holes in their nose with sticks stuck through. Some had small teeth made up in different styles and stuck through their nose and feathers in their hair and beads on their neck and pieces of shells cut out and put in their hair. Some had breast plates and bracelets and a band round their waist, two inches wide."

Mr. Bourne made an interesting entry in his logbook for

41

October 18, noting that they went looking for wood on shore at Duke of York Island and found one white man there.

October 19 "Mr. Bourne and some of the crew went ashore to see about anchoring. When they didn't come back, I was worried. It was getting dark. I thought they had been molested by natives." Three lanterns were put up in the rigging. They returned unharmed with some nice water which had come down from the mountain.

October 20 "The natives hurrahed when we let the anchor go. I saw eight little huts on the beach made out of bamboo and leaves with only a small space for them to crawl in. They were built very low.

October 21 "It looks so pleasant to see the green all around us. It seems as though I must go right among it." It had been over two and one half months since Annie had been on land.

October 22 "We went for a sail. Daniel said if we could find an island with no natives on it, we could land. We saw coconut trees on one island and we were afraid that there could be natives, there. So I fired the pistol and did not raise any but I frightened the little birds very much. We filled up on coconuts. When we returned to the ship, the decks were full of natives. The men drove them forward and took me right up in the boat and I got out on top of the cabin and then had to go down into the potato pen. Then I went right below to dinner."

October 23 "Daniel brought me a pair of pigeons but one had both legs broken so he had to be cooked. We put the pig in the birdcage with the other pigeon but soon found that they could not live together and had to part them."

The fine weather continued. Daniel and Annie were able to do their wash. They saw several islands, including Groene (unable to find) and Bouka (part of Papua New Guinea and the Solomon Islands group.)

One day the natives arrived wanting to trade their tortoise shells for axes and tomahawks but there were none on ship for selling. "If Daniel had had those items, he would have gotten $500 worth of shells." One cannot but wonder what the tomahawks would have been used for.

October 28 "We have gone east as far as we shall go and are now heading to New Ireland." They had had no oil since June 18 and were patrolling the whaling grounds of the South Pacific in their continuous search.

By early December, the weather had deteriorated. "I guess I should not have slept much if I had not had a swinging bed."

Their food situation was becoming worrisome. One day, when cook ordered the beef from one of the casks, it was discovered that the hoops had burst. There was much concern that their beef supply had rotted. Luckily, it was still edible. Annie took the opportunity to look down to where the casks were stored. "I had never seen it before. There were pieces of iron as large as my body which were used for ballast."

It was Annie's second Christmas at sea. Their cabin boy "tiptoed down the stairs and wished me a 'Merry Christmas.' Everyone was looking out to wish me that, first. We have had a beautiful day. But, I have not felt well. I have been taking out my white clothes and airing them and I am making Daniel a Masonic Flag." Daniel was a member of the Free and Accepted Masons.

They saw grampuses (dolphins), finbacks and small fish. Despite an obvious attempt to keep up her spirits, Annie misses her family. "I suppose they are having nice times at home, now. I wish I was there to enjoy it with them."

On New Year's Day, 1873, they sighted the island of New Guinea.

Finally, their luck changed. In mid-January, they saw a large sperm whale going no particular course at 11 am and three boats were lowered. Daniel originally joined the hunt but returned to work the ship down to the whaleboats. At 3 pm, the men struck and by 6 pm, the whale was made fast along side of the ship and all hands were aboard safe. "The whale looked very large as he lay along side." Once again, the deck was filled with constant activity as the crew began cutting in the blubber, boiling the pieces and finally storing the precious oil. For seven months, they had all been waiting for the hard won success of this day.

They met up with Captain Howland of the Kathleen who brought them seven New Bedford papers and a bunch of bananas. Several days, later, Annie went up on deck to enjoy the bright, pleasant day and to read the papers. "In the first one that I took up to read, I saw the announcement of my own dear father's death. No one can ever know how I felt reading that. After I got over the first terrible shock, I found that no pen can

43

ever describe my feelings." Nothing more about this loss was recorded in her journal. Did she think of her father as he stood on the distant shore waving his good-byes on the day she departed? It must have seemed an eternity since that happened. Little did she know, then, that would be the last time that she would ever see him.

Often, when people set off for new horizons, they expect that their loved ones will remain unchanged, just as they left them. Annie's father's death may have been a reminder to her that this was not always possible.

The search for whales continued to consume the thoughts of everyone. Nothing else was important. One day, a small group of whales was sighted in the distance. Daniel immediately sent out the boats after them. The crew did succeed in securing two irons to one of the whales but then several others got entangled in the lines and, in the end, all of them got away.

Chapter 8

On February 19, Daniel and Annie decided to visit the king in Salibaboo. "I carried the king's wife one of my dresses and cut her out another while ashore. I should think there were two hundred people standing around me. They made a great time of it."

Little did they know that as so often happened when they were near land, several members of the crew ran away. They left Salibaboo and headed for the Island of Kabruang where Daniel wanted to get some men to go to sea with him to replace the crew members who had deserted.

While at Kabruang, several visitors came on board the Tucker. Annie notes that she "flew around and fixed up a little." There was a missionary and a Dutchman. In the midst of all this, fourteen crew members tried to escape. Daniel was on shore trading with the natives. When he learned about the deserters he sent a German with a note for Mr. Bourne that he was to let him have three pairs of irons.

Back on land, Daniel and the German went after the escapees. When they returned, "Daniel was an awful looking man. His face was all scratched up and his hand all done up in a cloth. His white pants that he wore were as black as could be with mud. He had on a long black native dress (in place of the other clothes he had worn). He sent a boat right after the men that they had caught. In one and a half hours the boat came back with some of the men."

Of the fourteen deserters, only four had been caught. Annie writes: there were "the cooper and Fish and Bradon and a Portuguese that we call Mary Young who had fallen down a precipice and was hurt very badly. He was rolled up in a blanket and laying in the bottom of the boat. The German stopped and took dinner with Daniel and then bid his goodbye. Daniel, then, picked out his men that he wanted out of a lot of the natives that were on deck wanting to go with us. In about half an hour, the ship was underway." Nothing is recorded as to whether the deserters were punished.

On the first day of March, the Tucker anchored off Ternate and the harbormaster soon came aboard. Daniel and Annie went ashore to visit Captain Edward and his wife, who were going to a ball at the Resident's house in honor of the captain and officers on board of a Russian man-of-war which had been docked for some time with most of her crew sick with a fever. "We had an invitation to go with them, and I sent off for several things that I wanted aboard the ship. So, we made ourselves ready. Daniel, in black clothes with a white vest and I, in white. We had a very pleasant time. There was music and dancing. And refreshments, several times in the evening. The house was lit up very brilliantly and all along the roads the whole length of the pier making it look very pleasant."

March 5 "Today, Daniel bought me a silk dress from one of the officers aboard the Russian man-of-war. It came from China."

One experience they had in the middle of March demonstrated the need to be watchful when around natives. They had been at sea for many days when they noticed that they were being followed by a large pram which was in sight all day. "When the natives came alongside, we could not understand them. Some of our natives could. They said they were lost." But their boatsteerer threw an iron. Luckily, he missed.

There were several whale sightings but they continued to be illusive. "There was a nice lot of whales but they were very sly."

March 25 We passed Birds Island "which is a very prettily-shaped island. It is quite high and perfectly round. This forenoon, we saw a very large water spout and it was right in our wake. Daniel changed the course of the vessel as it came towards us so very fast. He had all the sails taken in. Mr. Bourne loaded a bomb gun (sometimes used against whales) to fire if he came near enough. It got within a mile of us then it began to go off. I never saw anything like it. It boiled up very high. I could see the large spout come down from the cloud. It was a grand and an awful solemn sight."

The quality of their food supply was again deteriorating. "For dinner, today, we had chicken soup flavored with cockroach and my tea was flavored with spider."

Another challenge was the weather. "We have had all kinds." One day, a chicken fell overboard. They lowered a boat and picked her up. In about a half hour, she was overboard, again, and they, again, had to pick her up.

One day, when Daniel and Mr. Harris went aboard the Kathleen, "I thought I wouldn't go as it looked as though it would rain. Mr. Folger, the mate, came aboard of us and, in the evening, we had a nice time playing backgammon. About 9 o'clock, it commenced to rain very hard. I went to bed at twelve o'clock. It rained so hard that Daniel did not come aboard and Mr. Folger had to stay aboard of us."

"It was still raining, the next day. Mr. Folger and I had another game of backgammon. The Kathleen was no where to be seen, when the mates came on deck. They went up aloft and after a while, saw a sail and ran for it but it proved to a proa (sail boat). In a short time, they saw another sail which was the Kathleen." One can only imagine what Annie must have been thinking when the ship on which her beloved husband had been visiting was no longer visible. But Annie wrote nothing about her fears.

"About 9 o'clock, we were near enough together so that the boats could go (back and forth) between the ships. Mr. Folger took leave of us and Daniel and the captain came aboard of us. It was so stormy. The captain stopped with us until ten minutes to nine in the evening. I was very soon in bed after he left."

April 4 "The sailors have been making rope. Daniel has been sawing out a bracket and I have been embroidering. I have got so tired of thinking. It is all I have to do - sit and sew and think."

April 9 "Just as the bell struck for ten o'clock, they raised whales from the masthead. In less than half an hour, three boats were down. Daniel acted as shipkeeper and stayed at the mast all of the time. It rained and was squally all day. At one o'clock, they lowered Daniel's boat and went after the whales that the mates' boats had captured. There were two dead whales which had been left with wafts (identifying markers) in them. At half past two, Daniel's boat came back with one which they made fast alongside. It was a small one, a calf. Then his boat started back for another. By three o'clock, two more whales, quite good size ones, had been brought alongside. At half past four o'clock, the boats were in their cranes and all aboard, safe. I could not help feeling thankful that nothing happened to anyone." It was the first successful hunt for the Tucker since January.

The weather improved and the crew continued to cut in the

whales and run the try works for several days. "Everything is greasy and smokey and has such a disagreeable smell." But, no one seemed to mind. Least of all Annie.

When their work was finished, the men scoured and cleaned the ship. "It looks nice to see the casks on deck full of oil. But there is not much of it, only about twenty-five barrels." They would need much more before they would be able to head home.

The next day, they sighted a large merchant vessel. Annie was hoping to send letters home but when Daniel signaled the ship's officers, they made no reply. "She was a Dutch vessel going through the passage at the south end of Celebes. She had a good breeze so we gave up thinking about sending letters. These merchant men don't like to be troubled with letters as a general thing."

While they continued their search for whales, they saw porpoises and the Tiger and Bear Islands. Daniel set the men to taking everything out of steerage so that it could be white-washed. When it was finished, "it looked white and nice."

As Annie's second year at sea drew near to a close, two events happened almost simultaneously - the first, caused much sadness and the other, a good deal of consternation. There were very few of the hardened crew members who had not come to enjoy Annie's dog, Fido. But Fido was sick, "so sick that I did not do much but hold him and try to ease the pain. He has been a very sick little thing all day and it made me feel very bad to see him suffer so and I not able to relieve him. As he cannot live, I shall be glad when he breathes his last and gets through his suffering."

The boat steerers took care of Fido so that Annie could sleep. "Daniel went up on deck, this morning at five o'clock, and our little pet had just breathed his last. One of the steerers had him in his arms rubbing him when he died. After breakfast, Daniel put him in a little box, then filled all in around him with sand and nailed the cover on. He lashed it up with rope and we buried our little pet in the deep, blue sea."

April 26 "This morning, before we were up, we experienced an earthquake. We were sound asleep but the vessel shook so that it woke us both up. She trembled like a leaf. We all thought she had struck. Daniel was out and on deck before I could say a word. The mate said he heard a noise that sounded like thunder at a distance. It did us no damage."

In the first week of May, almost two years to the day since it left New Bedford, the A.R.Tucker dropped anchor in Birma (Burma) Bay in Southeast Asia. There was no wind so they were not able to get up close to the other vessels moored, there.

It was a sunny, warm day and Annie must have been very excited as she set out in their small boat toward the shore. But, landing proved to be very difficult because the tide was out. In the end, Daniel had to climb out of the boat onto the back of one of his crew to be carried to shore. Annie stayed with the boat as it was rolled to the beach on rollers.

Daniel's first task was to stop at the commandant's office in order to submit the necessary landing information regarding the ship and its crew. It had taken so long to get in from the ship that there was no time to explore. And, when they began their journey back, they discovered that it was going to be even more difficult than their arrival. They had to be carried to the boat over the shoulders of four natives on chairs fitted with bamboo rails. "It was quite a way. The natives were up to their hips in water."

A few days later, they went to visit the king who lived in a very large house which was in bad condition. "It was about eighty years old. At the entrance to the yard, was a large building with long stairs to go up and see all the island. We did not go up. Around the house and outside the fence, there were men who squatted with their guns to guard the house. There were four canons mounted outside of the fence.

The king is only eight years old and lives there with his mother, his father having been dead some six years. He never is allowed to go out of the house until he is eighteen years of age. Then, he can go where he pleases." It's to be wondered if Annie compared the young king's restrictive way of life to Daniel who had already been to sea and traveled the world by the time he was sixteen.

The next day, "we went to the Mahomet Church. It was a large building. They would only let us go in as far as the middle because they are going to have a feast day, next Monday, to celebrate Mahomet's birthday.

But I must tell about the church. They have no seats, only three mats spread down in front of the altar where they kneel to worship. The men and women do not worship together but have a curtain drawn across one end of the room where the women go. They had a large well in the yard and two large stone jars that they keep filled with water. They sit on one side of the church steps and all have to wash their feet before going into the church."

On Sunday, Daniel arranged a special trip to one of the island's popular tourist attractions. "The grotto was quite a curiosity to me where the sea had washed in and formed shelves, one above another. The natives had made a little seat in the stone. There were a great many names painted all over of people who had visited, there. We carried paint to paint our names but Mr. Bourne mixed it too thin. I painted Daniels but it was very faint. While we were there, I saw snakes in the holes all around in the rock. I saw the heads of two peeping out to have a look at us. Also, I saw a snake skin where he had shed it. After sitting on one of the shelves and having a rest, we went back where we landed and spread the tablecloth on the grass for a lunch. We had wine and all. The dinner tasted beautiful, after tramping around and getting so very tired. The tide was so low, our sailor boys had had to carry us ashore in their arms.

After resting and taking some tea, we went for a walk to where they were making ornaments for the feast. There was a pyramid of flowers made of bright colored paper and a number of sprigs of flowers. On top of the pyramid was a pineapple made of paper. It was very perfect and looked pretty by lamplight. They were playing music and the natives danced for us. We had chairs brought for us to sit in. It was really interesting to see them dancing with their long knives. They call them creases and they were dressed very curiously. We sat and looked at them as long as we cared to. Then, we went back to the fort for supper."

The next afternoon, they went over to the town to watch the feast-day procession. Over three hundred men raced by on horseback. The roads were lined with people as far as they could see. At one point, a house was carried by on the shoulders of many natives. It was about fifteen feet square and made of bamboo and covered in cloth in the same colors as the United States flag - red, white and blue. Inside were four men and four women, all dressed in bright colored costumes with crowns of gold and silver paper, making them look glorious in the sun.

"The ladies danced inside the house, holding a fan and a pocketchief. After they finished, the house was set down and the four men got out dressed in fancy pants and skirts with sashes. They played on a small drum and two other instruments shaped like fish horns. I have never seen anything like it. There were three horses that danced with their riders on their back and they were dressed in great style."

On another trip ashore, they visited the family of a Chinese merchant. Annie was entranced by the tiny cups and saucers which were used to serve tea. "They did everything they could to entertain us and wound up a music box so that we could listen to its beautiful sounds." Annie, like her hosts, loved beauty whether it was found in a teacup or in music and she especially enjoyed sharing it.

Chapter 9

Shortly after their visit to the Chinese merchant, the A.R. Tucker took advantage of a fair breeze and current and was soon out of sight of Burma. In a rare comment, Annie writes that she "layed down after dinner and had a rest." She seemed to be having some problems with her health. Although she seldom mentions this in her journal, there was another time, two weeks earlier, when she wrote, "Daniel did my washing this morning. He would not let me do anything towards it. I was feeling so miserable." Perhaps, the many years at sea were beginning to take their toll.

May 16 "This morning, the watch killed the ox we got in Burma and we had some for dinner. It tasted very nice. I can see the Island of Celebes."

Soon, they were in the "Maccasser Straits" (Makassar Strait), which is located between the islands of Borneo and Sulawesi in Indonesia. "I can see Celebes and three small islands but there is no name to them on the chart."

One warm day, the steward killed a goose for dinner. "I have been stripping the feathers that came off him for a pillow. I made a pillow case and put the feathers into it."

Whales were sighted, early one morning, at the end of May. Daniel joined in the hunt and struck a small one. In all, four whales were taken, two of them quite large. Everything went perfectly and the whales were fastened alongside, cut in and the try works started by late afternoon. Oddly enough, not a shark was seen through all the cutting in. That night, it was especially calm with hardly a breath of air. Already, the deck was covered in grease.

May 31 "About five, this morning, Mr. Vanderloop came to our state room window and woke us up. He said that one of the men, named Bradon, had cut his finger off in the mincing machine. Daniel jumped right up and went on deck and found he had cut it off from the end of the finger to the second joint. Mr. Bourne got up and went on deck and he and Daniel concluded that the rest must come off. So they gave him ether and cut and sawed it off. It was the forefinger of his right hand."

The next day, Sunday, started off very pleasantly. The last of the blubber was in the pots boiling when Annie went on deck.

Between 10 am and 1 pm, whales were sighted from the masthead. By 1 pm, the boats were lowered and Daniel, his officers and crew set off after the whales. At 6:30 pm, Mr. Harris came alongside and brought a whale. Then he went to where Mr. Bourne and Mr.Vanderhoof were struggling with a whale which was "acting very bad." Mr. Harris helped kill the whale.

"Daniel did not get back to the ship until 25 minutes to ten. We did not get to bed until 11:30 pm. But, we went to bed feeling quite nice with three whales alongside." Almost as an afterthought, Annie added, "It has not seemed much like the Sabbath."

Finally, Annie was able to do some much needed laundering. "It has been so greasy all the week that I thought I could not wash. We have been stowing down the oil. The last three whales made us 30 barrels."

The very next day, more whales were raised. "I could see them very plain off deck." While the weather turned rainy, Annie watched as first, Mr. Bourne and then, Mr. Harris came alongside, each with a whale. In less than a week, five more whales had been captured and brought alongside. It looked as thought their luck had improved.

Another Sunday but, according to Annie, "it doesn't seem much like a Sabbath on our decks, this morning. Everybody is as busy as bees in a hive. At 9:20 am, two whales were cut in on deck and at 10:30 am, they were boiling." Even though there was little time for rest or even to eat, both Daniel and his crew continued their hard work, knowing that each barrel brought them that much closer to a successful finish to their journey. The last two whales made them 25 barrels, more.

The whale hunts, the greasy work of preparing the oil and the rainy weather made it very difficult to do laundry. One fair day, Annie took advantage of the weather to catch up but just as she hung the last piece of clothing to dry on deck, black clouds rose on the horizon. The skies opened up and rain and wind attacked her neatly hung wash which ended up wetter than when she had hung it.

While Annie was trying to do her wash, sperm whales were sighted in the distance. Black clouds rising in the north soon shut in the horizon so that nothing could be seen and when it began to rain, the men lost track of them. "While raining, the whales went we don't know where."

That night, Annie kept waking up with the sensation of something crawling across her skin. Sleep became impossible. As soon as it was light, she was up and looking through the bed. It didn't take long to discover the cause of her discomfort - cockroaches several times the size they should have been. "The boy and I cleaned everything out of my room. We did not find only three large ones."

As they neared the island of Borneo, a very large merchant ship came into view at a distance of about six miles. It was near the end of June and Annie was excited. "I was so in hopes that I should get the chance to send a letter home but my hopes were dashed for we have such strong winds."

The next day, however, Mr. Bourne was able to take letters aboard the merchant ship, Templer, out of Boston. Annie sent the captain a package of books. She found out that the vessel was bound to New York, had been to Manila and was carrying a cargo of hemp and sugar. She sailed under Captain Fessenden. "The captain was very kindly. He took my letter and said he would post it at his next stop where he was going for recruits. He sent me a large package of books and papers and a jar of preserves, some sweet potatoes and Irish ones. He also sent an invitation for us to come aboard, tomorrow, Sunday and spend the day."

Even though the next day was calm and pleasant, Templer had put too much distance between them for Annie and Daniel to visit. "Our friend was fifteen to twenty miles off, much too far to go gamming."

July 4 "Another month has rolled by. I suppose, today, they are having a celebration at home as it is the glorious Fourth. We had baked goose and all the fixings for dinner. That was the only celebration we could have."

For several days, the weather was very rugged, making it difficult for both Annie and the men to do their work. She especially had a difficult time trying to iron the new dress and wrapper she had made. The ship was listing back and forth and keeping the iron on the board was very difficult.

July 14 Daniel decided to take advantage of the wind and head straight for Singapore. "Today is my birthday. I am thirty-
54

two years old. I hope that I shall not have to spend more than one more birthday aboard this vessel." Annie must have had mixed feelings about her life at that time. Most certainly, she enjoyed being with Daniel, seeing places with names she had never heard and meeting people that she did not know had existed. But, she had been away from her family and loved ones for such a long time. Also, though she never mentions it, she must have been acutely conscious that her chances for a child diminished as she grew older.

During the next several days of good weather, everyone on board the Tucker was busy cleaning and repairing. Annie took all of her clothes out of the press (a chest or wardrobe in which clothes are stored) and aired them. She also fitted a black silk dress and finished another. And, she did her laundry. The men were kept busy scraping the ship which they then scoured with soap and sand and painted. Daniel painted their room. And, the cook worked hard at cleaning the galley. Annie also bound round a piece of carpet to put down in her room on deck. "The vessel begins to look very nice with only one coat of paint. We are 172 miles from Singapore and shall soon be there, if we can only have a breeze. I shall be so glad when we get there so I can have my letters from home. I can hardly wait to get them."

Singapore is an island located at the southern tip of the Malay Peninsula, 85 miles north of the equator. It is the smallest country in Southeast Asia. The British East India Company established a trading post, there, in 1819. Before that, the main settlement was a Malay fishing village at the mouth of the Singapore River. It soon became an important stop along the spice route and one of the most crucial commercial and military centers of the British Empire.[12]

Annie rejoiced in the "beautiful, fair winds" as the crew continued painting the exterior of the ship. A new spinnaker was installed. Daniel had the slop cask out and "the boys had a great time getting clothes to wear ashore." (Clothing was wrapped in bundles and shipped in casks stowed in a compartment at the end of the lower deck.) At about 4 pm, they saw the first lighthouse. "It was a long way off and looked like a tall straight stick." An hour later, they saw a large steamer astern of their ship. By this point, they also had a clearer view of the lighthouse. They were heading right for it.

The next day, it was cloudy as they lay at anchor waiting for the pilot to bring them into Singapore Harbor. When he came aboard, Annie noted that he was Malay. It then began to rain and continued to do so for five hours. "It blowed a perfect gale of wind." At noon, the wind died down. They weighed anchor and set sail. As they headed into that busy port, two steamers passed by them heading into the harbor and two more, coming out. They dropped anchor between 8 and 9 pm.

Chapter 10

They were forced to anchor further out than planned because "the wind left us." "In less time than I can write it, two boats were along side with runners who were very social gentlemen."

At 5:30 pm, Daniel went to shore with the runners, to find out if there had been any mail. When he returned, "I got two from Mother but not late ones, one from Mrs. Brown and another from Carrie Spooner. There was also a letter from Burma. "It was written in duck and, of course, we could not read it." There were several different newspapers including some foreign ones. Even a few that contained comics.

There was much excitement when two "Chinamen" came to the ship with clothes all ready and bolts of cloth. Then, a shoemaker arrived followed by someone else with all kinds of dress goods and shawls." Annie doesn't mention buying any of these offerings.

July 27 "Husband and I went ashore. We took a carriage at the pier and went over to New Harbor where they have built a new pier, lately. It was a very pleasant drive. We drove all over Singapore, mostly to see the sights and sights I did see. I saw so much that I hardly know what I did see."

They went to visit a Chinese church. "It was worth seeing with its many images, paintings and gilt work." After a day of sightseeing, they returned to the ship.

(Singapore is a country of many religions including Buddhism and Taoism. A smaller percent, mostly Chinese, Eurasians and Indians, practice Christianity. The Malays and some of the Indian and Chinese population are Muslim.)

Early, the next day, Daniel went ashore. While he was gone, a boat came alongside with trays full of shells. Annie bought a few pieces of coral and some shells. "I gave 25 cents for them" There were also several Chinese with different kinds of goods. "One of the China-men brought something in a cage that looked like a kitten only it had a very long tail." Daniel had already had a pair of shoes, some pants and a coat made while ashore which were delivered.

Later in the day, when Daniel returned he told Annie that he had arranged for a room at one of the hotels and that she could go ashore either that night or in the morning. Annie didn't waste

57

any time, "I was soon ready with my large trunk on deck. We got into the boat and were quickly alongside the pier. We took a carriage for the Hotel De La Paix, where we found everything nice and comfortable."

At the time that the Ricketsons disembarked in Singapore, it had been a British crown colony for several years. As such, it was directly under the Crown. Approximately 100,000 people lived there.

The next day, Daniel left the hotel, early, on business but was back for dinner at 1 pm which, they learned in Singapore, was called "Tiffin." That afternoon, they went shopping at two large stores. At Littles, Annie bought some needles, a net for her hair and some elastic. They returned to their hotel at 6 pm, just in time for tea.

August 1 "Daniel bought me a pretty breast-pin. Then we went down to Mericans where he is doing some trading to see if they sent the canned meat to the ship. He had ordered a present for me, an album cover of Sandalwood, which was supposed to have been sent to the ship without letting me know anything about it. But, one man brought it out who didn't know anything about the plan." So much for the surprise but Annie didn't seem to mind.

One experience Annie and Daniel had that week must have been very sad for both of them. "We went round and tried to get baby's picture taken to the photographers and the painters but it was faded so bad, they could not take it." Maybe, that's why, Daniel went out and bought Annie a special gift, a "beautiful little gold watch" which he told her was for her birthday present.

Mr. Bourne visited them and he and Daniel went for a ride, together. Daniel didn't return until quite late. Annie went to bed "but could not sleep on account of a rat that was in the room."

One beautiful morning, Daniel decided not to go aboard the ship until after breakfast. But then he did not return for Tiffin. He did not get back until 4 pm because he was very busy shipping men for his crew. When he did return, Annie made herself ready. They got into the carriage and went for a ride out of town about four miles to see a fresh water lake that supplied all of Singapore with water. "It is led through pipes under ground. It was a beautiful place."

Although Daniel was still busy shipping men, he took time to buy Annie a feather fan, a knife, some muslin and an underwaist. For himself he bought a clock and a pistol.

August 15 "Daniel did not go aboard ship, all morning. Mr. Bourne came ashore early and stopped to Tiffin with us. After dinner, Mr. Harris came ashore. He had had some trouble with the men running away. I went into one of the lady boarder's rooms and stopped most of the forenoon. Mr. Bourne had brought my pictures and albums and I carried them down for the ladies to see. They had a fine time looking at them."

On yet another shopping trip with Daniel, Annie purchased "a little lace and some muslin to go around the bed. Daniel bought a beautiful picture." After Tiffin, Mr. Bourne, Mr. Harris and Daniel went off in a carriage. When they returned, that evening, he and Annie "took a turn on the esplanade." After dinner, "we went down on the veranda. There were eight or nine gentlemen and three of us ladies. One elderly gentleman played the guitar, very nicely. I did not leave until 11 pm. Daniel did not come up until after midnight. One of the gentlemen, an American captain, gave Daniel his picture."

Daniel was on his way to settle up some of his bills when he encountered Mrs. Wilcox walking along the street. He told her that he was thinking of returning to sea and suggested that she call on Annie. As a result, both she and Annie had an enjoyable visit.

When Daniel returned without any letters for her, Annie was very disappointed. "I felt so bad not getting any late letters and had to cry a little." After Tiffin, she prepared to go on board the ship.

They had been in Singapore almost three weeks and Daniel was anxious to get back to sea. There was trouble with the men and he worried that more of them might try to run away. While they were docked, thirteen men had deserted. All of them were the natives who had been taken on at Salibaboo.

As they reached the dock, the Dubash, a government official, was waiting. With a flourish, he presented Annie with an intricately carved camphor chest. It was a perfect gift to have on board to store their belongings. Everything was put into the sampan which carried them out to "the old bark."

After the busy and social life of Singapore, it must have been difficult to settle into the everyday monotony of the shipboard routine. The next day, August 17, Annie writes, "The Sabbath day seems very long. It is so still aboard the ship, no ringing of bells or singing of birds as on shore. I have been reading some and went to bed and had a nap to pass the time away."

There were more problems with the ever-present cockroaches. Daniel had been helping Annie take her clothes out of the press to put away a picture and a bracelet when they found "any quantity of cockroaches. I had the boy take all my clothes on deck and shake them out. I also broke out one of the lockers and put some items away. I was very tired by dinner."

The ship was traveling through the Straits of Sunda which connects the Indian Ocean with the China (Java) Sea. They passed Borneo, the third largest island in the world, and stopped over briefly near Angier, Java. It took five hours for the boat to get them to shore. "We had a long pull of ten miles. Four natives paddled and the bonan (member of an ethnic group) who steered was an old native. I was very tired before we even got there." They stayed just long enough to trade for vegetables and fruit and to see the town. The piazza was very quaint and well maintained. Unfortunately, Annie acquired an unwanted souvenir of their visit - wet paint on her black silk dress when she leaned against some freshly painted railings.

Back on ship, Annie spent some of her time sewing. "I put some wristbands on a shirt for Daniel and worked on some worsted." While she was so occupied, the crew chased after sperm whales but they were quickly gone. One day, she saw a top sail schooner, two islands, unnamed, and a frigate.

Near the end of September, they were close to the Seychelle Islands in the Indian Ocean. Annie was frustrated that she was not able to wash because the wind was so strong. They saw plenty of fish and a finback but "Daniel made up his mind to leave these parts as we have seen no whales." They would go round the Cape so "my going ashore at Mahe (the largest island in the Seychelles) is all over."

The quick changes in weather that often happened at sea occurred one day as Annie was sitting and talking on deck. "All of a sudden, breakers were right close. We were right into them. By 8:30 pm, there was such a time as there ever was on deck. Daniel was hollering for the men to do this and that. He called all hands and such a running to and fro, and hauling of ropes. As good luck had it, the ship tacked the first time in good shape or we should have gone on the reef. We were all very much frightened but everything worked well and it was daylight, that being in our favor. But those great white rollers coming toward us did not look very nice. Little did we think, when we sat so comfortable talking, that we were in so much danger, going into danger as fast as we could. One breaker broke under our stern and another under the bow. I could see bottom under the starboard boat. We did not go to bed till quite late."

The next day, it "blowed harder than it has since we left home. Daniel had the side boards put in round the skylight and an old canvas laid over the top. He also had the doors in the gang way sheeted over. It made it very dark and gloomy below in the cabin. I had my lamp lit all the forenoon. I went up on deck but my little room, there, was all wet and Daniel did not think it safe for me to stop in it for a sea might come over and take it away. I had my canary and cockatoo carried down and hung in my state room. I did not care to stop on deck in such weather. We lost four ducks and five chickens. They got chilled and died. Some of the rest, we put in the galley to get warm and now they are in tubs. Tonight, steward got the supper set on the table and the vessel gave one of her dives. Most everything went on the floor. We lost most all the hash. We did not break a dish but it was quite laughable."

Chapter 11

Although the weather improved, the next day, Annie decided
to take a nap after dinner. Almost, instantly, she heard the cry,
"Hard down the wheel!, Hard down the wheel!" She ran up on
deck to discover that while the men were putting up a new sail, a
"colored man" had slipped from the mast and struck on the
starboard boat. "He never knew anything after he struck that
boat. He went right down like a stone into the water. I think he
must have broken his back or ribs. It was an awful fall. I heard
him when he struck. Daniel had the wheel put hard up and the
main yard hauled back but he went right down. It was a terrible
thing to think of a man being sent into Eternity without a minutes
warning."

The man had joined the crew at Singapore. His home was at
St. Helena where the Tucker was headed. "But," as Annie
recorded, "he has gone to his long, long home. The work goes
on as though nothing had happened but the countenances of
everyone look sad. This evening, though, I heard some of the
men laughing and talking forward as if nothing had happened."

Later that week, Annie discovered that the cockroaches were
back. She was checking on clothing in the drawers of her
cabinet and found that they had eaten the lining out of one of her
favorite pieces. "I had to rip it up and fix it all over."

One especially stormy night when the ship rolled and pitched
about, Annie was taken sick with what she describes as wind
colic. "Daniel stayed up two hours with me. He had the steward
make a fire and get hot water and I got easy after a while."

The next day was a fine day made even better when sperm
whales were sighted. Annie watched as the boats closed in on
them. "I saw one whale put his nose out of the water. It was
about the same length as the ship. I am so pleased to think we
have got a little more and hope this day will only be the
beginning of getting a lot of oil." In all, three whales were
captured.

They were still in the Indian Ocean and passed the island of
Madagascar. "It looked very long although we could only see a
part of it."

During the third week of October, the crew was kept busy
fitting the mainstays and getting the anchors on the bow. The

ship was headed to St. Augustine Bay for wood and water.

As they entered the bay, a canoe came alongside with two natives, a boy and a man. "The man has his hair all done up in round bunches of dirt, grease and clay. His is the most comical looking head I ever saw. They both wear cloth thrown over their shoulders and down to their knees."

The anchors had just been dropped when more canoes began to come from every direction. Soon the decks were full of natives. Most of them were drunk. "There are schooners laying here and I suppose that is were they got their rum."

Although the weather continued pleasant, the natives kept coming on deck. The men were busy getting wood and water on board, all day. It was difficult because they had to work with the tide and contend with the natives.

One day, two schooners headed out of the bay. "Daniel and I got up on the potato pen. Daniel waved his hat, I my pocket-chief as they passed us. We hoisted our flag and ran it up and down saying good-bye. They did the same. One of the captains fired two guns as he passed us."

From the natives, Annie bought a little straw hat and some tamarinds and lemons. "Daniel and I squeezed them and put the juices in bottles."

By the end of the month, the natives were gone. Annie was able to do a wash and put up a few tamarinds in sugar. The men had all the wood and water aboard that was possible and all of it was stowed down. "It is very discouraging we have so little oil."

On one trip to shore, "we went down to the Frenchman's and he was trading with the natives. Iron, pots, beads, knifes and razors for beans. He had some fifty or sixty bushels heaped up that he had bought. One of the natives had a tiger's tooth on a string round his neck and he took it off and gave it to me. He shot the tiger himself and two more before that one. We stopped a while to see the Frenchman and trade with the natives. Then we bade him goodbye as the boat had come for us."

On October 31, they left. "I was so glad to get out of that place. The natives were so noisy on deck and there were so many of them. I have been picking up things and put some limes in jars, wrapped some lemons in papers to put away."

After days at sea, Annie was excited to see a ship. "She came right across our bow. She gave us her longitude by holding up a board with it marked on it. We gave them ours, the same way."

On November 13, they rounded the East Cape of Africa to the South Atlantic and were headed to the island of St. Helena. When she saw it, two weeks, later, Annie thought, "It is very high and looks as though it is nothing but rocks." The island was formed by volcanoes.

Once on shore in Jamestown, the island's only town, at their hotel, Daniel and Annie met up with Captain and Mrs. Allen from the bark, Falcon. Annie wanted to shop, first, and then to see the island. "At 10 am, the carriage was at the door to take us out in the country to see Longwood, (Napoleon's home in exile), and his grave. We had to go way up on the mountainside. It looked very steep and dangerous to look down from such a height. We first came to where Napoleon was buried, some three miles this side of Longwood. It was a very pretty place, down in a valley. A large, marble slab lay on the ground with an iron fence around it. Then, another fence enclosed quite a space of land and some pretty trees. One willow stood near the grave. It was a very quiet, pretty place."

(Napoleon requested to be buried on the banks of the Seine in Paris, France. He was originally buried on Saint Helena in an area called "Valley of the Willows" in an unmarked tomb. When Annie visited his grave, his remains were no longer there, having been moved to Les Invalides in Paris in 1840.)

After their visit to the grave, the two couples drove on to Longwood and toured the house. "There was a lady, there, that went with us. Her husband had stood guard over Napoleon's grave. There is nothing pretty about the house, outside. It is a low, old fashioned house but, inside, it is very nice with large, airy rooms and a great number of them. Where Napoleon breathed his last was a bust of him sitting on a monument with three large wreathes of everlasting flowers put there by the French. We went out into a little flower garden. It was full of weeds, no care taken of it. On one side of the house, was a small pond built round with stone where he used to keep his fish."

Previously, while they were driving to Longwood, they had stopped and ordered dinner of ham, eggs, boiled cabbage, Irish potatoes, bread, butter, cheese and watercress. It was ready for them on their way back. After dinner, Mrs. Allen and Annie took a walk over to a small church where there were several graves in the graveyard.

They then rode ten to twelve miles to the consul's residence which Annie found "very pretty, so cool and nice." After refreshments, they rested before continuing on to their next visit with a Mr. Fitman who was expecting them. He was 72 years old. "This part of our ride was more dangerous. We had to go so near the edge of the precipice. No one looking at the barren, rocky ridges could imagine there was so much beautiful scenery. As soon as we passed Munden Point, Jamestown appeared suddenly between the rocky precipices, 1000 feet high. The white buildings with the green foliage gives a pleasing effect to the scene. It was very picturesque and we enjoyed it very much."

They also enjoyed the carriage ride. "Our carriage was very comfortable. Mrs. Allen and I sat on the back seat and Daniel and Captain Allen on the front seat which was high. The driver sat on one of the horses and we had a man that went behind the carriage to open and shut the gates and to put the top up when the sun was too hot."

They were quite tired when they returned to their rooms but the day was not over, yet. "This evening, after tea, a local resident, Mrs. Pooley, and her daughter came in to pass the evening and her husband had the band play out in the front of the house. He, being the leader of the band, had to stop out there till they were through playing. They played several pieces for us, "Old Lang Syne" and "Hail" and "Yankee Doodle". It was 11 pm when we retired, tired enough."

Their last day, Daniel and Annie went to the picture gallery to have their pictures taken to send to their parents. "A young lady took them. Her father was dead, he used to take them but now she does to help support her family."

They had spent only two days on St. Helena. More than likely, Daniel was anxious to return to his search for whales.

One day when at sea, Annie saw a large ship bound southward and a brig going in the same direction as The Tucker. "About 11 am, she was quite near so Mr. Bourne took a boat and went aboard. Her name was the S.E. Voohres under Captain W.H. Fulford, only 37 days from New York. She was bound to Mariritius and Calcutta loaded with petroleum oil. The captain sent me a large bundle of books, papers, some late, a beef tongue, four cans, two of corn and two others."

These gifts did little to cheer Annie who writes, "I am feeling miserable, today, and have been most sick. I have been abed for several days."

On December 21, Mr. Bourne took a boat's crew aboard a brig, a Spanish vessel where not one person could speak English. "He was able to find out the longitude and carried ours with him. But, he did not stop for long for he could not talk to the captain. I sent a bundle of papers but Mr. Bourne did not leave them, as no one could read them."

On Christmas, Annie reported, "There has been nothing the last two days to write about but I cannot pass Christmas by and not have something. I gave Daniel a present of a cigar holder that I got for him in St. Helena. He was very much pleased with it for he had wanted one for a very long time. Daniel had a hog killed so we had roast spare-ribs for dinner, Irish potatoes, stuffing and stewed pumpkins.

Later that day, we raised whales and saw them jump out of the water, once. But it was so rugged, we saw nothing more of them. We thought we were going to have a nice Christmas present.

We also saw two barks. One came across our stern so near that we could see the men very plain on deck. They waved their hats. Daniel had one of our boys hold up the longitude marked on a board. The captain of the bark got over the side and marked his longitude. She was painted black so we could see it plain."

Finally, the next day, they raised whales at 9 am. Three boats gave chase and at 11 am, all three boats were fast to their whales. The third mate, Mr. Vanderloop's line parted from the whale. Since the first mate, Mr. Bourne, was fast to a very large whale, he went to assist him. But the whale threw his jaw over the boat and took out a large piece of it. The boat capsized, leaving all the men in the water. Fortunately, no one was hurt or lost but then Mr. Bourne had to cut from his whale to pick up the men. The boat was stoved in in two places and all of the oars were knocked out of the boat except for two. The second mate, Mr. Harris, saw that there was trouble. As his whale was dead, he put a waft into him and concentrated on towing the boat alongside the ship. Then he went right back after his whale. The others got the remaining boat on deck. Mr. Harris' whale was a

66

very small one. The men went right to work and cut him in.

January 1, 1874 "And, here it is New Year's again. So they pass away - year after year, each one bringing us nearer our home." The weather was pleasant but became quite rugged after dinner. "I had a little present for Daniel that I had been making and had not quite finished. I thought I would finish it while he was at the masthead and give it to him after tea but he must go down and look for his account book in the drawers and found it. It was a shaving tidy and I had bought a shaving brush to put in it. We had considerable fun about it for several of the men knew that I was making it and they had said that he would find it before I got it finished. Daniel was very pleased." Later, she and Daniel cleaned out a trunk and a chest. They found a lot of cockroaches in among Annie's clothes - not the best way to start off a new year.

Later, that week, they invited Captain Allen and his wife, aboard. Their ship, the bark, Falcon, had anchored, nearby. "I began to fix up a little for company. It was a beautiful day. We spent a pleasant day with them. I had quite a number of things to show Mrs. Allen. We had some patterns to cut and any amount of talking to do as we were some acquainted having been on St. Helena, together. Daniel had a pig killed before they came. Our friends bade us, goodbye, about 10 pm, giving us an invitation to come aboard on Friday, if the weather were good.

The next day, Annie was busy putting things away and fixing some clothes to wear on her visit to the Allens. While sitting in her little room on deck fixing a pair of stays, she had several pains in her right shoulder. In the beginning, she did not think that they were anything to worry about. But, when she went to bed, that evening, the pain had become so bad that she woke Daniel up. "I could not stand it any longer for every breath I drew seemed as though I could not bare to draw another. Daniel put a chair in the bed and fitted me in it as easy as he could but nothing would relieve the pain. He got something and rubbed me with it. I was still awake at 4 am when Daniel gave me a few drops of laudanum. I slept a little but it was not a good sleep for I was talking and laughing, Daniel said. In the morning, I tried to get up and dressed and, with the help of the boy, to get my room to rights. I couldn't eat breakfast and came near to fainting away and had to go back to bed."

Daniel sent a message to The Falcon to tell the Allens that Annie was sick. Captain Allen sent some books. Mrs. Allen sent two kinds of cake, a dish of bananas put up in sweet pickle and a string of eggs. She also sent a little pink stone from Annabona, Africa.

Mr. Williams, a mate on the Mattapoisett which was also anchored, nearby, came to visit with books and papers. "I was very glad to see him because he had seen my dear Mother only seven months before and could tell me something about her."

It was not unusual to have so many ships anchored in whaling grounds. And, aside from the chase, their proximity provided excellent opportunity for gamming, visiting back and forth.

One cloudy and chilly day, Annie decided that she had rheumatism in her shoulder. She was miserable. But despite her ill health, she kept busy working on a chair seat while Daniel made a trunk cover.

During the second week in February, the men called Daniel because they thought they had seen the light of a ship. But it turned out to be the lighthouse on Cape Frio, on Brazil's southeast Atlantic coast. Only one whale was taken that month.

March started off blowing a gale. "I have not been on deck. I had the teethache, all night. My face is swollen all out of shape and I am feeling most sick. I layed abed, part of the day. I shall be so glad when next month comes for we shall go ashore and I shall get some letters."

Annie spent her days working on a watch case and a little work chair for her mother. Daniel set in silver in a jewel box. One evening, six little pigs were born. On another day, Annie made sure the boy cleaned out her room on deck. Daniel painted the woodwork all white and the floor green sprinkled with white. "It looks very nice and clean. I cleaned out my drawers in my stateroom and bound round a little piece of carpeting to put down in my room on deck."

April 5 "A bark hailed us, they had lost their way and Daniel gave them the course. They were all colored aboard. We told the captain with our signal flags that we could see land. He thanked us and changed his course to go along with us. We were both heading to Barbados."

Chapter 12

On April 6, the Tucker dropped anchor in the harbor at Bridgetown, Barbados. The tide was running strong and a squall struck which forced them into an English schooner, the Lena of Brixham. We "carried away their jib-boom and damaged their figurehead, which was that of a lady and slightly hurt her in other ways. Considerable damage was done to us, our jib-boom was carried away and one of our boats, stoved in. The stern was also hurt. I was very much frightened. The steward helped me below. Daniel went aboard the other vessel to see the damage. And, after breakfast, her captain came aboard us." No further mention is made of this incident either in Annie's journal or the ship's log.

Despite their problems during arrival, they landed, checked into a hotel and then headed right away to the Icehouse where both Daniel and Annie savored the taste of ice cream. Annie was delighted to receive a letter from her mother, another from her friend, Rebecca, one from Daniel's mother and several newspapers from both her mother and from the Wings. "I did not get to sleep until quite late for I had been through so much and then having so much news from home."

The warmth of the Barbados sun must have been a much appreciated antidote to the dampness of the ship. And the colorful flowers, the sound of the birds in the swaying palms, a welcome relief to Annie.

The next day, Daniel took Annie to Whitefields Store to get some things for the concert they were planning to attend. "I got a very pretty blue and white dress skirt. It was poplin and looks very much like silk. I also got a hat to match and blue ribbon for bows, as well as a lace pocket-chief and a braid for my hair." Back at the hotel, Annie was kept busy hemming frills for the white blouse that she wanted to wear. After attending the concert, Annie noted that it was very good but poorly attended and that they were back at the hotel between 11pm and midnight.

Despite Annie's rather unusual life, she was still concerned about fashion. For that reason, on the Sabbath, she did not go to church with Daniel. "It was not because I did not want to go but I had nothing that was nice enough to wear. They dress very stylish, here." Annie was not about to be seen, wearing the wrong kind of clothes.

One evening, the Ricketsons went to the theater. "One of the colored servants went with us and carried the sun umbrella over my head and my fan and glasses. Then she came for us when it was done about 11:30 pm."

Just before leaving Barbados, Daniel took Annie shopping. They went to DeCostas and bought a carpet for a center rug. Captain Dickson of the bark, Atlantic, who was going directly to New York, said that he would take their purchase and then send it on to New Bedford by express. They had the carpet rolled up in oilcloth and sewed up in canvas. At the same time, Annie also sent a short note to her mother. Daniel gave the ship's captain three dollars for his services.

While they were in Barbados, Daniel had 7,711 gallons of oil shipped back to New Bedford. Unfortunately, eleven men, including the steward and the cooper, deserted.

They set sail on April 23, a little under two and a half weeks after they arrived. It had been close to three months since they had taken a whale.

They sailed past the island of Martinique and stopped at the island of Dominica to replace the deserters. At 5 pm, a "colored" gentleman, Mr. Riviere came aboard for tea. It was a beautiful moonlight night, when he took his leave.

Their new friend had invited them ashore to his home which was only a short distance by horseback. "It was very cool, there, and we enjoyed ourselves very much. We had dinner about 1 pm of fresh meat soup, then fried meat, cabbage, fried cakes and preserved wines. In the afternoon, we went out for a walk and saw a peacock, a very pretty one. The mills were only a little way from the house where they make the sugar."

Mr. Riviere proved to be a very helpful friend when, during her visit, Annie developed a strange condition in which her face swelled up out of shape. He called it, Erysipelas. She was given some rum to bathe her face but was feeling so badly that she and Daniel said goodbye, mounted their horses and returned to the town.

The next day, Annie could not see out of one eye and the other was almost closed, her face was still swollen and she was broken out all over. Mr. Riviere brought her a bowl of chicken soup but she was not able to eat it. There is no record of what her affliction was.

By the end of May, they were, once again, at sea. Now in the North Atlantic, on May 24, they met the schooner, Ellen Rodman. Captain Gillette who was from Fairhaven came aboard and took tea. He brought a late shipping list and some Standards and stayed until 1:20 pm. Annie had a bad cold and went to bed. Her health seems to have deteriorated during this last part of her voyage. She spent her time writing to Daniels's father and mother.

They continued their search for whales and eventually took one which yielded thirteen barrels of oil.

On the first day of June, they sighted a bark. Daniel got the Tucker's latitude and hoisted the flag to let those in the other ship know what country they were. "Up went his flag. He was Spanish and he hauled back his mainyard so Daniel thought he perhaps wanted something. He sent Mr. Bourne who stopped only a short time. He could not talk with the captain who could not speak English. His mate could speak a few words. The captain sent Daniel some cigars and me some guava jelly."

June 5 "The beautiful Bermuda light was seen last night. At 4 pm a pilot boat came along side but we did not want his services." They did not go ashore until June 15 and only stayed a couple of days, according to the ship's log.

During the last week of June, they raised sperm whales. By 9:30 am, three of the boats were lowered. At 2 pm, they returned with no whales. Just as they were taking up the last boat, one of the boys, George, raised whales, again. The boats were again lowered and Daniel joined them and took one whale. At 3:30 pm, he returned and made it fast. At 4:45 pm, the other boats returned and were put up on their cranes. The men worked at setting up the staging and preparing for the work, the next day. "All are very cheerful and carrying smiling faces."

The next morning, all hands were at work in the grease when Annie went on deck. "They did not get the case in last night so this morning they got it up to bail it but the sharks had been helping themselves through the night. They only got half a tub full."

On the second of July, a very serious incident took place which could have resulted in a mutiny. Daniel and Annie were

71

seated at the table, when one of the men told Daniel that some of the men wanted to speak to him. When he went on deck, he learned that five of the men were refusing to work. They said they did not have enough to eat. It was definitely a bad situation and Daniel needed to react quickly in order to prevent it from getting worse. He immediately ordered all five of them to be put in irons. One of the men soon begged to come out. He was willing to work. Daniel let him out. There is no mention of this incident in the log and no further discussion of it in Annie's journal.

On July 16, they raised the whaling schooner, The William Grozier, out of Provincetown. Captain and Mrs. Roberts invited Daniel and Annie aboard. They went over at 11 am and stayed until 11 pm. "We had a very pleasant time." They had not met with the captain or his lady before but that made little difference and they were well acquainted in a short time. The Roberts gave them a lot of reading material and some canned fruits.

Early the next day, Captain and Mrs. Roberts came aboard the Tucker, and stayed well into the evening. "We learned each other's different kinds of work and she enjoyed looking at the different things that I had bought and had been given me. I gave her some baskets and shells and a pail, some wool and canvas."

July 19 "I have been reading all day. I have a toothache, very bad. Daniel took out a little piece of it. I put laudanum on it, then oil of clove, which stopped it but the root is there and it is ulcerated. It makes my head feel very bad."

A few days later, while the men were mending the sails, they raised a wreck. Daniel and Mr. Bourne boarded it and brought back some copper but it was not very good. Mr. Bourne said that there were chains hanging to her and that they looked new. Perhaps, it was a slave ship and one cannot help but wonder what happened on board that deserted ship.

One calm, beautifully clear day toward the end of August, Daniel and Annie, for a short time, were able to forget their cares and responsibilities. They went fishing. It was a great time. "Daniel caught two fish and I caught four. But he lost one overboard."

Their enjoyment quickly ended when Daniel saw two ships in the distance, both with their boats down. This could only mean that there whales in the area. Immediately, they returned to the ship and Daniel and Mr. Bourne both went up to the masthead and called all hands on deck. It was 3:30 pm when three boats were lowered. Daniel, his officers and crew began the hunt. From her viewpoint on deck, Annie watched as Daniel, Mr. Harris and then Mr. Bourne each got fast to a whale.

Without warning, Daniel's whale took off past the stern of the ship to windward so quickly that both the whale, Daniel and his crew were soon out of sight. Mr. Bourne, knowing that Daniel's boat was out of sight, wafted his whale and then pulled to the ship as fast as he could. He climbed back on board and began to work the ship to windward. Next he ordered someone to take over the wheel so that he could climb the masthead. But he was not able to raise the boat.

"I hardly know how to describe the night. The sun went down and we could see no boat. We set the side light, put the lanterns up in the rigging and at 9:15 pm sent up a rocket and, again, at 10:30 pm and another at midnight. Except for the lights on the ship, all was in total blackness.

A little past 3 am, Annie heard Daniel's voice. It must have seemed a wondrous sound! "How thankful I felt to hear that voice again. I said 'good morning' to Daniel before he even got out of his boat. He had a whale and they made it fast. I never want to go through such a night again. Mr. Bourne was very anxious. He told me he would do everything that lay in his power to find the boat and he did."

Another greasy deck with the tryworks going and the men all working at trying out the captured whales. During all of this, they sighted the Cornelius Howland. Daniel, knowing that he would not be able to take care of all his oil, had a flag put to the main and another to the peak. The vessel soon changed her course and went right across the Tucker's stern. Annie got up on the potato pen so that she could see. Daniel had told her that he had once been on the Howland for a short voyage. The captain came aboard and Daniel asked him to take the two whale heads but he refused as he had blubber on his deck, too. He did not stay long but he left a bundle of late papers. He was only three weeks and four days from home. He left them a bundle of late papers including a few from New Bedford. Before returning to sea, he told them that he had been at home for four years.

August 30 "They had to cut from the head and let it go for

they found they could not take care of it. I felt bad enough for we want oil so bad. Oil is running on deck and the boys are scooping it up."

By mid-September, the weather had deteriorated. It was rainy and squally. "Both the sea and sky were lead color and such seas as came rolling up. I had a lantern lit and hung up on the skylight which was covered with canvas and tied down with ropes. Today has seemed the longest day to me of all that I have spent aboard this vessel. I had to be alone most of the time and am not feeling well. It is very close down in the cabin with everything closed. The time seems long, now, as it draws near for us to start home."

On September 18, the boats returned from another hunt without a whale. "We all felt very disappointed for we want one more to make us a good season's work."

On the twenty-third, they put up all the sails and started for home. There would be no more taking in the sails at night. "I shall be so glad when we arrive in New Bedford."

It looked as though Annie was going to get her wish for just one more whale to make a good season's work. A whale was sighted, one morning, but just as the men were about to set out, a squall came up. The whale was only about one half mile from the ship. But it rained so hard that you "couldn't see a ship's length off."

In about one and one half hours, the weather cleared and, in a short time, the whale was sighted again. Three boats were lowered and soon the whale was struck. By 1:30 pm, the boats were alongside with their dead whale. The crew made it fast and then got ready to start cutting. By 5:30 pm, it was all on deck. And so, Annie was granted her wish for one more whale for a good season's work.

In the middle of the night, Mr. Vanderloop woke Daniel to tell him that there was more trouble with the men. Daniel jumped out of bed, did not stop for any clothes and went right on deck. Mr. Bourne, hearing the noise went up, too. They put one man in irons. "He was going to cut one of the men with a spade and was very saucy to the third mate. It gave me quite a start as I was sound asleep."

Annie began packing, knowing that her three and one half year journey was almost over. Feeling tired, she decided to go on deck. Soon, "from aloft, I saw a red apple floating in the water." Surely, that meant that land was near. She must have welcomed the sight and the pleasant thoughts it aroused. Perhaps, she remembered the apple trees at neighboring farms, of how, in spring, their pink blossoms laced the ground. Or how, now, in the fall, their leaves were ruddy and gold. Or she thought of her mother as she bent to lift an apple pie from the oven, of the pleasure on her face as she served it to her loved ones.

The crew was readying the ship. All morning, they put lime over the decks. After letting it lie throughout the day, they then gave them a thorough scrubbing. They are nearing home and Annie hopes the wind will keep.

October 17 "A beautiful, bright sunshiny day. Two brigs passed us this morning and also a bark. We have got fair wind at last and, this afternoon, at 2 pm, we were 82 miles from Gay Head Light. I am in hopes that the wind will continue fair so we can go right along up the New Bedford River."

The end

1. Emma Mayhew Whiting and Henry Beetle Hough, *Whaling Wives,* (Boston: Houghton Mifflin Company, 1953), 143-44
2. Linda Grant DePauw, *Seafaring Women,* (Boston: Houghton Mifflin Company, 1982), 107
3. Ibid., 108
4. Harold Williams, *One Whaling Family,* (Boston: Houghton Mifflin, 1964), 10
5. Elmo P. Hohman, *The American Whaleman,* (Clifton: Augustus M. Kelly Publishers, 1972) 162
6. Harold Williams, *One Whaling Family,* (Boston: Houghton Mifflin, 1964) 31
7. John R. Spears, *The Story of the New England Whalers* (New York: The Macmillan Company, 1910) 209
8. William M. Daves, *Nimrod of the Sea* (North Quincy: The Christopher Publishing House, 1972) 89
9. Linda Grant DePauw, *Seafaring Women* (Boston: Houghton Mifflin, 1982), 140
10. Philip F. Purrington, foreword to *The Journal of Annie Holmes Ricketson* (New Bedford: The Old Dartmouth Historical Society, 1958)
11. William Berchen, *Bermuda Impressions* (New York: Hastings House, Publishers, 1976), 76
12. Encyclopedia Britannica, *Singapore,* on line

Bibliography

Amaral, Pat. *They Ploughed the Seas.* St. Petersburg, Florida: Valkyrie Press, 1978.

Ashley, Clifford N. *The Yankee Whaler.* Garden City, New York: Halycon House, 1942.

Berchen, William. *Bermuda Impressions.* New York: Hastings House, Publishers, 1976

Bockstoce, John R. *Whales Ice and Men, The History of Whaling in the Western Atlantic.* Seattle: University of Washington Press in association with the New Bedford Whaling Museum, 1986.

Chatterton, E. Keeble. *Whalers and Whaling.* Philadelphia: J.B. Lippencott Co.., 1926.

Davis, William M. *Nimrod of the Sea* or *The American Whaleman.* North Quincy, Massachusetts: The Christopher Publishing House, 1972.

DePauw, Linda Grant. *Seafaring Women.* Boston: Houghton Mifflin Company, 1982.

Druett, Joan. *Petticoat Whalers: Whaling Wives at Sea, 1820-1920.* Auckland, NZ: Harpercollins Publishers, 1991.

Goode, George B. *The Fisheries and Fishery Industries of the United States.* Washington D.C.: Government Printing Office, 1884-7.

Hall, Elton W. *Sperm Whaling from New Bedford.* New Bedford, Massachusetts: New Bedford Whaling Museum and The Old Dartmouth Historical Society, 1982.

Hohman, Elmo P. *The American Whaleman: A Study of Life and Labor in the Whaling Industry.* Clifton: Augustus M. Kelly Publishers, 1972.

Kugler, Richard. *New Bedford and Old Dartmouth; A Portrait of a Region's Past.* New Bedford, Massachusetts: Trustees of the Old Dartmouth Historical Society, 1975.

Olmstead, Francis A. *Incidents of a Whaling Voyage.* New York: D. Appleton and Company, 1841.

Ricketson, Annie Holmes. (Foreword by Philip F. Purrington). *The Journal of Annie Holmes Ricketson on the Whaleship A.R. Tucker, 1871-1874.* New Bedford, Massachusetts: The Old Dartmouth Historical Society, 1954.

Whiting, Emma Mayhew and Henry Beetle Hough. *Whaling Wives.* Boston: Houghton Mifflin, 1953.

Willliams, Harold. *One Whaling Family*. Boston: Houghton Mifflin, 1964

Spears, John R. *The Story of the New England Whalers*. New York: The Macmillan Company, 1910.

Whiting, Emma Mayhew and Henry Beetle Hough. *Whaling Wives*. Boston: Houghton Mifflin Company, 1953.

Williams, Harold, ed. *One Whaling Family*. Boston: Houghton Mifflin Company, 1964.

ABOUT THE AUTHOR

LAURA RICKETSON DOHERTY has lived all of her life in Massachusetts. She credits both her father and mother, Leonard and Mary Ricketson, for her early interest in writing. "My father had a very wry view of the world about which he often expounded and my mother entertained us in the wonderful oral tradition for which the Irish have long been known," she notes.

While a student at the University of Massachusetts in Amherst, she learned about the New Bedford author Daniel Ricketson and his friendship with Henry Thoreau. She was excited to find a photograph of the interior of his writing cabin which, she says, looked a lot like the way her father kept his papers.

Research had always been one of her special interests but learning when to stop has not been easy. She has written on diverse subjects for local and regional newspapers and national magazines. One article on the cemetery situation in the town in which she was living ran in *Boston Magazine*, much to the consternation of some town officials. The headline was "Dying to Get In."

Most of the research for *Annie Ricketson's Journal* was done at The New Bedford Public Library and the Kendall Library. For over a year, she consulted the original ship log of the *A. R. Tucker* as well as Annie's journal, shipping papers, newspapers, and well-documented books about whaling and life at that period. At the New England Genealogical Society, she was able to answer the question about her relationship to Annie. Her father and Annie's husband, Daniel, are both descendents of William Ricketson who settled in Massachusetts in the 1600's.

Currently, she resides with her husband in Duxbury, Massachusetts which is located on the coast, halfway between Boston and Cape Cod. She is a member of her local historical commission and cultural council and works at The Art Complex Museum.